LITERATURE & THEOLOGY IN COLONIAL NEW ENGLAND

LITERATURE
& THEOLOGY
IN COLONIAL
NEW ENGLAND

KENNETH B. MURDOCK

GREENWOOD PRESS, PUBLISHERS
WESTPORT, CONNECTICUT

The Library of Congress cataloged this book as follows:

Murdock, Kenneth Ballard, 1895–
    Literature & theology in colonial New England ₍by₎
Kenneth B. Murdock. Westport, Conn., Greenwood Press
₍1970, ᶜ1949₎
    xi, 235 p. 23 cm.

    "The substance of this book was presented in a course of lectures
given for the Lowell Institute in King's Chapel, Boston, in March
and April, 1944, as one of the institute's annual series on 'Current
topics in theology.' "
    Includes bibliographical references.

    1. American literature—Colonial period—History and criticism. 2.
American literature—New England. 3. Religion and literature.   ɪ.
Title.

PS195.R4M8   1970   810.9′001   78–104247
ISBN 0–8371–3990–2   MARC

Library of Congress   70 ₍7₎

Reprinted by Greenwood Press,
a division of Williamhouse-Regency Inc.

First Greenwood Reprinting 1970
Second Greenwood Reprinting 1976

Library of Congress Catalog Card Number 78-104247

ISBN 0-8371-3990-2

Printed in the United States of America

TO
Mark and Ruth

Preface

THIS BOOK attempts to outline the relation between the New England Puritans' fundamental theological ideas and their literary theory and practice. It is neither a treatise on Puritan theology nor a history of Puritan literature, and it makes no attempt to go deeply into the origins of Puritan methods and principles or the earlier influences which helped to determine their seventeenth-century form. It is primarily an essay on some of the ways in which ardent supporters of a particular set of doctrines sought in an important historical period in literature to express them; it deals with the colonial Puritans' successes and failures as, to use the word in its most general sense, artists. Like most honest men of ardent religious convictions they were eager to communicate their beliefs to others, and like all such men they faced the problem of finding appropriate artistic means. Puritan methods of solving the problem were to some extent peculiar to Puritans because they were dictated by their special religious and philosophical tenets. I have attempted no apology for them, and this book is not a defense of Puritan literary theory or practice. Indeed, my own view is that the principles which Puritan authors chose to follow, as well as the conditions under which they worked, commonly prevented their achieving artistic successes comparable to those of religious writers of other schools of thought. I have tried, however, to show that, for better or for worse, the Puritans followed a reasoned and mature literary theory, deliberately chosen in preference to others because it seemed to them adapted to the needs of their audience and in harmony with their whole intellectual scheme. Judged comparatively, by a reader whose religious and artistic sympathies are non-Puritan, the results were sometimes good and sometimes bad; but the concern of this book is less with praise or blame, although neither is excluded, than with an attempt to describe Puritan literary theory, to show how it worked, and to point out the relation between the special characteristics of colonial Puritan literature and those of Puritan thought. Such a study should bear directly on the fundamental question of how religious ideas are to be given adequate artistic expression — a question as old as theology and as modern as next Sunday's sermon.

Since my major interest here is in that question I have made no effort to go deeply into the theological intricacies of New England Puritanism. Those have been thoroughly explored in Perry Miller's *The New England Mind. The Seventeenth Century,* to which I am deeply indebted, and I have not tried to summarize his careful analysis or to rehash much of the material on Puritanism accessible in the work of other scholars. For my purposes it has seemed enough to stick to the theological fundamentals, ignoring many of the thorny technicalities which delighted Puritan ministers in their studies or in their public debates with their colleagues.

In so doing, I think I have done about what those ministers did themselves. Their religious system was the intellectual pattern of their universe; for the scholars among them every detail of it was fascinating; but the writings that impressed most readers, and probably seemed to their authors their most useful labors for God, treated not scholarly minutiae but a body of truth essential to every man who looked to God for life. The typical Puritan divine wrote more often for plain men than for pundits.

The substance of this book was presented in a course of lectures given for the Lowell Institute in King's Chapel, Boston, in March and April 1944, as one of the Institute's annual series on "Current Topics in Theology." My theme is, I believe, actually a "current topic," even though my material is the thinking and writing of men who lived more than two centuries ago and, for the most part, held ideas radically unlike ours. The problem of finding adequate literary expression for religious values is, as I have said, perennial; moreover, the Puritans' special approach to the question has in some ways, I think, affected the attitude of their successors. Furthermore, it seems to me plain that the times which produce major literary works on religious themes are those in which religion and theology are most alive. Conversely, when religious writing is flat, with none of the qualities of great art, when it is merely sentimental or sensational or deals largely in genteel platitudes, the age which fosters it is likely to be one in which religion is more a matter of sterile convention and surface emotion than of convinced faith. If this is true, an examination of the extent to which, for all their shortcomings, the ardently devout Puritan pioneers of New England succeeded as artists should serve to test not only some of their religious values but also certain of the qualities of current religious thought.

My debt to *The New England Mind* I have already mentioned. *The Puritans*, an anthology of Puritan literature, edited with introductions by Perry Miller and Thomas H. Johnson, has also been especially useful. William Haller's *The Rise of Puritanism* deals with English Puritans, but I have drawn upon it freely and gratefully, and much that I have written does no more than apply to colonial New England, and illustrate from it, the conclusions he has reached about the Puritan literary tradition in England. The other books which have contributed most are named in notes, which are intended not merely to show the sources of my material but to acknowledge my thanks to the scholars who have made it accessible.

The quotations in my text follow the cited sources except that in printing extracts from early writers I have not kept the long "s," have modernized "u" and "v," and have occasionally changed spelling and punctuation in the interest of intelligibility for modern readers.

It is a pleasure to express my thanks to the Trustee of the Lowell Institute in Boston, Mr. Ralph Lowell, for permission to use my lectures for the Institute as the basis of this book; to Eleanor W. Casey, Ellen Wiggins, and Edith A. Warren for their secretarial help; to Sterling Lanier for reading the proof; to Perry Miller for invaluable criticisms and suggestions; and to my wife for her constant aid in the preparation of both the lectures and the book. Finally, I have a special debt to Mark Schorer. He read and criticized my manuscript for the lectures, and his scholarship and literary expertness saved me from many errors I must otherwise have made. He has not seen the finished book, but any virtues it may have are, I feel sure, largely traceable to his patience in keeping me on the right track in the initial stages of its composition.

K. B. M.

Boston, Massachusetts
October, 1948

Contents

Contents

LITERATURE & THEOLOGY IN COLONIAL NEW ENGLAND

I

THE BACKGROUND: THE GOLDEN AGE
OF ENGLISH RELIGIOUS LITERATURE

THE Puritans who dominated the intellectual life of New England for the first century after the British settlement of Plymouth and of Massachusetts Bay achieved their domination and influenced later generations largely through the spoken and written word. They conceived of their colonial venture as a crusade to establish a commonwealth of God, and they saw that if they were to succeed they must find means to keep their supporters strong in the faith, to persuade the doubters, and to arouse the unawakened. Throughout history, literature, in the broadest sense of the word, had been an indispensable adjunct of Christian thought and life. No literature, of course, could by itself make a religion or give validity to a theology, but the Puritans must have recognized that no religion or theology had ever made itself a force among men without a literature of some sort. What would Christianity be without its Bible? Or Christian worship without words? Or the preacher's zeal with no means of communicating it? In their prayers the pious needed verbal symbols by which to express their feelings, and even those who held that God's grace might so work in a man's heart as to reveal

I

the truth to him directly, even the great mystics rapt in a sense of immediate personal communion with the Divine, had, it appeared, often tried to clothe their visions in words. The emphasis which the Puritan put upon learning and literature proves that in his view they were not decorations for the Christian life but essentials of it.

Inevitably, then, the New England Puritan read and wrote, and inevitably in so doing he ran into the old problem of how to give in words proper expression to divine truth. He failed often, he had his full share of weaknesses and blindnesses, and as an artist he faced special handicaps in the rigors and limitations of his life as a colonist. But he kept at his task, studied diligently both books and men, and ultimately created a body of literature which was, considering the circumstances, extraordinary in bulk and contained many pages of genuine artistic excellence. The best writing of early New England testifies both to the intellectual and moral strength of its authors and to the wisdom with which they chose, and the skill with which they used, rhetorical methods admirably adapted to express their conception of the essential beauty of holiness. That conception was in many ways too narrow to satisfy artists of other faiths, but even so no fair-minded critic can overlook the merits of the best writing in which the Puritans revealed it, nor will anyone at all interested in the methods of religious art fail to find illumination in their work. They were determined to communicate both the truth by which they lived and the beauty they saw in it, and they

must have realized that prose or verse which was careless or clumsy could not serve. Certainly they seem to
have schooled themselves in a way of writing which
was neither. Their work even apart from its intrinsic
merits is therefore indispensable material for any study
of how far and by what means theological ideas and
religious emotions may be conveyed through art.

From the point of view of such a study an understanding of the colonial Puritan writer involves first
of all some recognition of his attitude toward English
religious literature in his time. Some of it he read and
approved, much of it he suspected or disliked, but he
knew a good deal about most of it. It fixed a kind of
standard for his own work, since he could not refute
the books he found bad if he wrote more carelessly than
their authors and since he naturally took the works he
admired as models for content and style. What he
chose to learn from contemporary English writers and
what he liked and disliked in them are clues to the
principles he most steadfastly upheld.

The seventeenth century — more specifically the first
fifty years or so after the settlement of Plymouth — was,
in England, "the age of clergymen, the apogee of the
pulpit and of the great divines," [1] the "golden age" of
religious literature. The reasons why were many and
complex, and a full exploration of them would be irrele-
vant here, but some appreciation of a few of them is
central to understanding any religious writer of the
period, Puritan or Anglican, Londoner or Bostonian.

For one thing, the seventeenth-century artist was still

under the spell of the Renaissance. Its aesthetic stimulation, so splendidly displayed in the great Elizabethan poets and dramatists, still warmed him; he shared something of its excitement in the classics, and his temper of mind marks his kinship to the experimenting and inquiring humanist scholars of the Renaissance, English and Continental. He felt himself to be both the heir of the ages and a dweller in a period which could, as Francis Bacon put it, "far surpass that of the Graecian and Roman learning." He had confidence that what he could discover of truth for himself might be better than, or at least as good as, anything handed down to him from an ancient philosopher or delivered to him by the authority of any institution old or new. He agreed with Bacon that he should "esteem of the inquisition of truth as of an enterprise." [2] Since the "inquisition of truth" could not exclude "divinity" there was a new curiosity about the bases of theology, and, as an immortal by-product, a magnificent new English translation of the Bible.

With the humanism, the pagan love of beauty, and the intellectual curiosity of the French and Italian Renaissance, was blended, once the channel was crossed, a new spiritual seriousness. The English Renaissance was strongly tinctured by the mood of the Protestant Reformation. Obviously, then, the artist turned often to religion, and what he wrote — the King James Bible of 1611 or the seventeenth-century prayer books, the sermons of John Donne or Jeremy Taylor, Marvell's poems or the epics of John Milton — might mingle a

Renaissance delight in beauty with the Protestant reformer's zeal for religious truth.

Even more fundamental is the fact that the seventeenth century began in unshaken confidence that the universe centered on God and that religion was the heart of life. Theology was, therefore, the noblest of sciences. "Much of that curiosity about the world" which was strong in the Renaissance and "now sends intelligent people to psychology, science, philosophy, or biography was then satisfied within the field of religion." [3] When an artist wrote on religious themes he knew that his work was rooted in life, and his words had "the poise, the easy substance and assurance, of work moving in the main stream of its time." His books gained thereby "robustness" and "breadth," for which, says Helen White, "one often searches in vain in later religious literature." "Here is no thin diagram of possibility but the full round of a dominant view of the world." [4]

Another immensely important reason for the seventeenth century's becoming the great period of English religious literature is the fact that in a very real sense it was the time of the actual English Reformation. The separation of the English church from Rome under Henry VIII had been rather political than religious, and from Elizabeth's reign until the end of the seventeenth century England faced the problem of what English Protestantism was to be in polity and creed. High church Anglicans were content to stay close to the tradition of Rome; more moderate Church of England men went farther toward Protestantism in doctrine and in liturgy, but believed they should build not only on the Bible but on whatever in Catholicism seemed rationally justified and proved good by the experience of the past. But no Anglican could be complacent, for he had always at his heels a vociferous group of more extreme religious reformers, radical Protestants, who insisted that all that smacked of Rome was bad and that the Bible alone must determine all matters of polity and belief. These men differed among themselves about theological details and forms of worship and church government, but their hatred of Rome and their insistence on the exclusive authority of the Bible united them on major principles. They were the men whom we call, using the word in its most general sense, Puritans. The Puritans who settled Plymouth represented one sect; those who made the great migration to Massachusetts Bay, another; the Presbyterians who for a time were a dominant party in English seventeenth-century politics, a third. Some Puritans never deserted the English Church but tried to reform it from within. Others, like the settlers at Plymouth, separated themselves completely from it. But however much one Puritan group differed from another, all agreed well enough on some essentials of an extreme Protestant position to be critical both of Rome and of Canterbury. The result, of course, was tension and a stimulus to probe into the bases of essential Christian doctrine. In trying to define its Protestantism, Protestant England had to reckon with profound social and political cleavages, since both the established church and the established government were involved. Only a man virtually blind and deaf could sit apart in smug indifference to theological and ecclesiastical debate. Henry Osborn Taylor once wrote: "The spiritual force animating a new religious movement attracts the intellectual energies of the period, and furnishes them a new reality of purpose." [5] English Protestantism in the early seventeenth century was still in a sense "a new religious movement," since its final form and goal had not been settled and experiment and controversy were rife. And Mr. Taylor's statement is true, probably, not only for religious movements which are "new," but for any that are active. Whatever else religion and theology may have been in the decades after 1600, they were certainly active — so active that they helped to bring on and carry through a great Civil War, to populate a large part of a new continent, and to remodel the lives and thought of thousands of Englishmen. Small wonder that they attracted "the intellectual energies of the period" and that most of the best minds of the time, and most of the best artists, turned at least on occasion to writing of religion.

Thence came volume after volume of controversy, Biblical exposition, verse, pious meditation, and sermons. Of the whole mass, of course, much failed artistically. Theological controversy and exposition then as now were written with an eye to clarity rather than to beauty, and there were then as now plenty of devout and learned men deeply moved by faith who never found words for what they felt. But, on the other

7

hand, a surprising number of Englishmen in the seventeenth century preached and wrote with such richness of literary effect that their books are alive even though many of their specific doctrines are forgotten or have fallen into disrepute.

The transplanted Englishmen who preached and wrote on the shores of Massachusetts Bay were, it must be remembered if they are to be understood at all, extreme reforming Protestants — Puritans, in common parlance — and it is just as important to remember that most of what now seems best in the religious literature of their day in England was written by devotees of the English church. The Puritan in Boston might protest, and did, that he was not separating himself from that church, or the best of it, but in fact his opposition to the Laudian high-church movement and to what seemed to him its Arminianism made him distrust Anglican ritual, a good deal of official Anglican doctrine, and, naturally, most of what Anglican writers wrote. The New Englander, therefore, commonly could not appreciate — and did not emulate — the best "divine poems" or "holy prose" of his day in England. Instead, the current English books he turned to most often were those of the English Puritans, and those books usually differed markedly from the work of the seventeenth-century Anglican or Catholic.

They did so in large part because of the difference between the Catholic and the Protestant attitudes toward the senses, toward material objects which appeal strongly to them, and toward the use of such objects in worship.

The difference is important for any study of religious literature because literature deals with the senses, with the felt texture of life. Religious writing may be concerned with the most intangible reality, with the most transcendental or ineffable truth, but it must transmit some measure of feeling or the words remain lifeless on the page. Logic, clarity, and explicitly defined terms may do very well by themselves to expound a moral argument or clear up a knotty theological dilemma. But true religious experience, a sense of God, a faith in divine beauty, a vision of essential Christian holiness, demand more for expression than logical structure and the accurate use of words in literal meanings. The religious artist, in other words, may write in prose but needs the genius of poetry. It is when his writing moves as well as teaches and stirs his readers imaginatively that it becomes art, and it is only then that it comes near to what is for a man of faith closest to the heart of reality. It has been said that "in great measure the inspiration of art has been religious ecstasy" and that "art is a form of worship." [6] This may be challenged, but it is surely true that insofar as religion is a matter of inner experience, of faith as opposed to mere knowledge, it requires imaginative means for its full expression.

As John Livingston Lowes put it:

Whatever else religion may be, it involves the attempt somehow to grasp the unseen and that which we designate as the eternal. But the unseen and the eternal . . . must, in order to be intelligible to finite minds, be translated into terms of the seen and the temporal . . . The essential element of all poetry

9

which has religious significance is precisely that imaginative
transformation of the unseen which is felt to be eternal into terms
of things which we have heard, which we have seen with our
eyes, which we have looked upon, and our hands have handled.
Just that it is . . . which underlies the central doctrine of
Christianity, the profoundly imaginative conception of the
Incarnation . . . the supreme translation of infinite into finite,
of unseen into seen.[7]

In art the translation is achieved by the artist's imaginative power, by his ability to find ways, whether he writes
poetry or prose, to make spiritual emotion and experience comprehensible to flesh and blood.

All this, in its essentials, the Puritan artist seems to
have understood quite as well as the Catholics or Anglicans. No more than they could he suppose that religious literature would be effective if it excluded all
sensuous appeals and all imaginative insight and dealt
only in cold fact or lifeless formalities of logic. He
understood man's nature better than that. Therefore
the literary attitudes of the three groups — Puritan,
Anglican, and Catholic — differed not so much in kind
as in degree. The question was to decide just what
sensuous material was proper in religious art and how it
could be fittingly presented. On that the Catholic and
the Puritan positions were far apart.

The Catholic "sees a ladder of ascent from beautiful
things to beautiful minds and beautiful souls, and,
finally, to that unchanging Beauty which is, if not God,
then in God." He "sees the Incarnation . . . as a
sanctification of the body and the senses." [8] Or, more

simply, Catholicism "has persistently affirmed that, as the body, the senses, the affections, and the imagination are integral parts of man, they must all collaborate in God's service; that the lower may officiate as instruments to the higher." [9] So, in Catholic worship there is an attempt to appeal to the eye, the ear, to all the senses in some measure, and in much Catholic literature a frank use of sensuous material not simply as an illustration of the divine but as valuable in and for itself. The result may be bad at times. There are possibilities for sensationalism, for sentimentality, for concentration solely on the material. The religious symbol, the object of sense, "may become materialised, and superstitious reverence is the result." [10] But with all its dangers, the admission of the great body of concrete and sensuous material, almost without restriction, as fit stuff for the religious artist opens to the Catholic writer a generous treasury of resources.

Richard Crashaw, an English Catholic poet writing in the days of the first settlement of Massachusetts, may serve as an example. Take first four stanzas from his "On the wounds of our crucified Lord":

> O these wakefull wounds of thine!
> Are they Mouthes? or are they eyes?
> Be they Mouthes, or be they eyne,
> Each bleeding part some one supplies.
>
> Lo! a mouth, whose full-bloom'd lips
> At too deare a rate are roses.
> Lo! a blood-shot eye! that weepes
> And many a cruell teare discloses.

O thou that on this foot hast laid
Many a kisse, and many a Teare,
Now thou shal't have all repaid,
Whatsoe're thy charges were.

This foot hath got a Mouth and lippes,
To pay the sweet summe of thy kisses:
To pay thy Teares, an Eye that weeps
In stead of Teares such Gems as this is.[11]

Here is a poem of religious devotion, but here are roses, gems, mouths, kisses, and full-bloom'd lips. For some readers the emotions called up may be too close to the flesh to savor of religious devotion and too sensual to evoke an instant spiritual response. But to Crashaw, and to most good Catholics of his time, such a reaction would have seemed strange. Love, even in terms of a "sweet summe" of "kisses" from "full-bloom'd lips," was the essence of their emotion toward our crucified Lord, and there was no gulf fixed between the love felt by lips and mouths and that by the aspiring soul. Or take the most-quoted lines in all Crashaw, the conclusion of one of his poems to St. Theresa:

O thou undanted daughter of desires!
By all thy dowr of LIGHTS & FIRES;
By all the eagle in thee, all the dove;
By all thy lives & deaths of love;
By thy larg draughts of intellectual day,
And by thy thirsts of love more large then they;
By all thy brim-fill'd Bowles of feirce desire
By thy last Morning's draught of liquid fire;
By the full kingdome of that finall kisse
That seiz'd thy parting Soul, & seal'd thee his;

By all the heav'ns thou hast in him
(Fair sister of the *Seraphim*!)
By all of Him we have in Thee;
Leave nothing of my SELF in me.
Let me so read thy life, that I
Unto all life of mine may dy.[12]

Here too there are "lives and deaths of love," "fierce desire," "the kingdom of a kiss." But Crashaw's emotion is real, and the sensuous images, the rhetoric, and the music convey it inescapably. The reader may protest against it, but the lines may still make him feel, which in such a case is perhaps better than to know, what it is to love a spiritual ideal to the point of complete absorption in it. Crashaw, like other Catholic religious writers, may often be too luscious, too perfumed, too sensually — or even sexually — evocative for Anglo-Saxon tastes, at least where religion is concerned, but it is worth remembering that his best poems, and the best of other Catholic writers, have power to stir the reader to an actual and intense physical experience of the emotion which the author feels in the presence of the divine.

If, as one Catholic critic puts it, we have been made "ashamed and frightened of sense and sex in religion," and "if spirit is simply the negation of sense, we must of course condemn . . . Crashaw." "But this," asserts Mr. Watkin, "is a false philosophy, doubly condemned by the doctrine of Creation and its fulfillment, the Incarnation . . . If God is indeed closer to the soul than one human being to another, and united with her in the

13

supreme mystic union more intimately than soul with body, religion must be essentially nuptial — the physical nuptials of earth its least inadequate reflection and image." The entire man must live in religion "with that intense life and concentrated experience that we call ecstatic. If religion is too 'pure' to afford this ecstasy, man will turn elsewhere." [13] Father Ellard, in his book on the Catholic liturgy, makes the same point. "Only Catholicity," he says, "gives full play to the needs of bodily as well as spiritual homage." "Redemption was accomplished by *God-in-the-flesh*; in keeping with that dispensation, the Wisdom of God established a religion in which *things of the spirit* are constantly linked with *things of sense* . . . God will catch up fallen humanity — but as by the cords of the New Adam, that is, by sensible, material objects and forms and symbols." [14] So the church building itself, the marble of the altar or Communion table, statuary, stained glass, wrought-iron and brass, tapestries and veils, linens and vestments, the carved crucifix, jeweled chalices, the poetry of the ritual, its music, the fragrance of flowers, the gleam of tapers, the sound of bells, the scent of incense, banners, palm branches, ashes of penance — "all these natural objects the Church has known how to emancipate and recruit as aids to sanctity, as subsidiary channels of Christ-life, as strands of the 'cords of Adam.' " [15] Augustine wept glad tears when he heard church music; he declared, "There can be no religion, true or false, without external ceremonial." [16] From the Catholic point of view the idea of " 'primitive simplicity . . . of Christian worship,' in the sense that Christianity ever rejected cult acts because they appeal to the senses" is pure myth.[17]

One more point in Catholic thinking on art and religion is expressed, again by Father Ellard: "The most elemental of all canons governing sacred music is that it is *addressed to God,* and not to man. To be true to its first law, sacred music must be meant for the ear of God. As such, it must be of man's very best." [18] The theory, here applied to music, holds for the other arts. "God stands in no need of human gifts; but, since men would avow their gratitude, express their aspirations and their homage, let them offer of their best." [19] Let them build and adorn cathedrals, let "the wit of the poet . . . be consecrated to God; *le jongleur* may perform his feats of agility to honor the Queen of Heaven." [20] And as other things appealing to the senses may be "cords of Adam" to elevate man toward God, so literature may not only be a fitting offering to God but a means of drawing men closer to him. "The wonder which poetry must produce may be not at the wit of its author but at the wit of God, at the fearful and wonderful nature of His creation." [21]

The more extreme the Protestant the more he disagrees with such Catholic thought, because he considers the senses as at least potentially "seductive — instruments of the flesh, enemies of the spirit." [22] Even recognizing the need of sensuous appeals in religious writing, he considers many of them — perhaps most — as possible sources of error, and so limits drastically his use of them in art. A reviewer of Lord David Cecil's *Oxford Book of Christian Verse* says, apparently with Protestant writers in mind, "Christian poets have tended . . . to recoil from the unguarded reality with which any poet who would speak the language of imagination . . . must grapple." [23] Lord David himself declares that the English Protestant poet "feels it profane to show himself in all his earthy imperfections before" God. "He will allow himself to express only unexceptionable sentiments, love, reverence, humility: will voice no aspiration save for a purer soul and stronger faith." "As for using any but the most decorous language to express his feelings, the very idea horrifies him . . . The writer . . . does not say what he really feels, but what he thinks he ought to feel: and he speaks not in his own voice but in the solemn tones that seem fitting to his solemn subject." [24] The tendency to write only out of the moral, respectable, rational part of the poet's nature came chiefly after the Reformation "when the whole realm of sense became increasingly suspect; . . . Protestantism . . . represented a split in the integrity of human experience." [25] Ralph Waldo Emerson, after hearing a Roman Catholic mass, wrote: "The Unitarian church forgets that men are poets." [26] A high-church Anglican said in 1941 that Protestantism "has thought of 'spiritual' as something opposite to 'material'; the latter is evil and can have no part in worship. Worship is a matter of the mind and soul; there is no place in it for . . . the beauty of nature or man's creation." [27] Such comments, as common among Protestant writers as among Catholics, could be duplicated many times. Most critics agree that strict English Protestantism — especially in its severer varieties — tends to distrust the senses and so to offer scantier materials for art than the tradition of Rome.

The reasons are several. One seems to be racial, arising from the characteristics of the British temperament, which inclines to be grave in its religious expression and to link piety with sobriety to the disadvantage of joy. This asceticism is, according to Miss White, shown in the fact that English works of devotion on the whole avoided the "type of religious symbolism and imagery" which was the "highly detailed and sensuous, often realistic presentation to the imagination of historic episode or vision or even dogmatic symbol, at its best an artistic performance of a high degree of imaginative power and emotional intensity." Such writing tried "to bring religious truth home not only to the intellect, but also to the imagination and the feelings," but Miss White points out that we have "positive evidence" of the British distrust of it, since those who translated Continental work into English "usually expurgated such passages." She cites as an example a section from the *Meditations* of Granada in a 1599 Protestant edition in English: "Consider, how he that clotheth the heavens with cloudes and adorneth the feildes with flowers, and bewtie, is here spoiled of all his garmentes," remains in an abridged form, but such sentences as "Beholde, how that roiall bloude distillinge out from his brayne, trickeleth downe all alonge by the heare of his head, and by his sacred bearde, insomuch as it watereth, and dyeth the verie grownde under him" disappear altogether.[28]

A second ground for the Protestant suspicion of the full Catholic acceptance of the senses in the process of worship was simply his dislike of anything Catholic. The extreme Protestant — the Puritan — on occasion carried his hatred of papist symbols to the point of downright vandalism. But even his gentler compatriots remembered the Spanish Armada, remembered that Spain was a Catholic power, and confused patriotism with prejudice against the Roman Church. An amusing hint of this comes in Crashaw, who felt he must apologize to his English audience because Saint Theresa was Spanish:

> What soule soever in any Language can
> Speake heaven like hers, is my soules country-man.
> O 'tis not Spanish, but 'tis heaven she speakes.[29]

The thoroughgoing Protestant of the seventeenth century thought that his distrust of the senses was based soundly in both theology and psychology. Sin had made the passions of fallen man hard to control.

> The senses are seduced by Objects, these help to abuse Imagination, which excites disorders in the inferior parts of the soul, and raiseth Passions, so as they are no longer in that obedience, wherein original Justice kept them, and though they be subject to the Empire of Reason, yet they so mutinie, as they are not to be brought within the compass of their duty, but by force or cunning.[30]

A New England poet complained that

> The Reasonable Soule doth much delight
> A Pickpack t'ride o' th' Sensuall Appetite.
> And hence the heart is hardened, and toyes
> With Love, Delight, and Joy, yea Vanities.[31]

Without going into the details either of the psychology or of the theology it can be said that the net result of a complicated process of thought was the conclusion that soul and body, spirit and sense, reason and the passions, were pairs of hostile forces. So we have George Herbert, the Anglican, writing that the nourishment and strength which are sent him by God can

> not get over to my soul,
> Leaping the wall that parts
> Our souls and fleshy hearts;
> But as th' outworks, they may controll
> My rebel-flesh . . .

Only God's grace can open "the Souls most subtile rooms." [32]

Clearer still are some lines of the Puritan Andrew Marvell:

> Earth cannot shew so brave a Sight
> As when a single Soul does fence
> The Batteries of alluring Sense,
> And Heaven views it with delight.
> > Then persevere: for still new Charges sound:
> > And if thou overcom'st thou shalt be crowned.

Fruits, flowers, downy pillows, soft plumes, roses, perfumes, music, fair women, gold, and worldly glory and knowledge are all listed among "the Batteries of alluring Sense" which the "resolved soul" must fight off in order to find the "everlasting Store" which lies beyond this world.[33]

The more firmly a religious writer stuck to this strain of Protestant thought, the farther he left behind him the Catholic theory that it was permissible to make frank use of sensuous material and to appeal to the senses in worship and religious art. Also, the more difficult he made his task as an artist. In Dean Inge's words:

> The Protestant, in his preoccupation with ethics, undervalues the aesthetic side of life, and thereby loses the sympathy of most persons who have the artistic temperament. Poetry plays a much larger part in life than the Protestant is willing to admit. For him a myth must be a hard fact or a wicked lie; sacramental symbolism is fraudulent magic; all the petty world of half-belief which the Catholic imagination spreads between the self and hard reality must be swept away ruthlessly.[34]

To this we may add that when the Protestant does this sweeping away he deprives the artist of material very useful to him if his desire is to communicate in terms of genuine emotion his sense of devotion, of faith, of the splendor and majesty of God, of death, of salvation, of redemption, or of any great divine fact. He may still write clear essays on moral conduct or rational expositions of theological doctrine, but his resources for moving men's hearts by literary means, for stimulating true religious feeling as opposed to mere understanding, are severely circumscribed.

Yet the Protestant established church of England in the early seventeenth century produced a religious literature unequaled in our language before or since, emotionally moving and no more concentrated on the communication of mere doctrine or theological wisdom than on conveying a living sense of religious experience. The explanation is that Anglicanism in the days of James I and Charles I was, in its attitude toward art as in so much else, a middle way. In ritual it kept much of the traditional symbolism and beauty. Music, vestments, richly decorated altars, and the beauty of words in the Prayer Book, were all used in worship. The Anglicans were Protestant in that they more than the Catholics emphasized the opposition of sense and spirit, but they were not Puritan in the liberality with which they admitted sensuous elements in the service of God. Wit, beauty of language, music, or architecture might all contribute in acts of devotion to Him. Like their Puritan brethren they felt that what appealed only, or too intensely, to the sensual side of man was to be avoided, but they compromised by using some objects of sense which the Puritans would have rejected as too "carnal" or profane in their associations to typify or illustrate the spiritual, and justified themselves by insisting that the sense images, the symbols of the poem or prose passage, were important not in and for themselves but only insofar as they illustrated or explained the divine or moved men to be receptive to, and to remember, God's truth.

A few passages from writers of the day should make the point of view plain. George Herbert, in his *Priest to the Temple*, has a charming paragraph on "The

Parson's Church." It is always to be neat. At festivals it is to be trimmed with boughs and perfumed with incense. Texts are to be painted on the walls, but the painting is to "be grave, and reverend, not with light colours, or foolish anticks." The Communion cloth is to be "fitting, and sightly," and the carpet "of good and costly Stuffe." [35] But the parson cares for all these things "not as out of necessity, or as putting a holiness in the things, but as desiring to keep the middle way between superstition and slovenlinesse, and as following the Apostles two great and admirable Rules . . . *Let all things be done decently, and in order*" and "*Let all things be done to edification.*" [36] Similarly, in his poem "The British Church" Herbert emphasizes the middle position of the Anglican in his attitude toward the religious use of the senses:

> A fine aspect in fit array,
> Neither too mean, nor yet too gay,
>   Shows who is best.
> Outlandish looks may not compare:
> For all they either painted are,
>   Or else undrest.
>
> She on the hills, which wantonly
> Allureth all in hope to be
>   By her preferr'd,
> Hath kiss'd so long her painted shrines,
> That ev'n her face by kissing shines,
>   For her reward.
> She in the valley is so shie
> Of dressing, that her hair doth lie
>   About her eares:

While she avoids her neighbours pride,
She wholly goes on th'other side,
And nothing wears.[37]

And a delightful figure from Herbert's "Man's Medley" makes vivid the idea that the sensuous, although not to be rejected, is subordinate to higher things. It is not forbidden, Herbert writes, that man in this world "Taste of the cheer," but he should do so

But as birds drink, and straight lift up their head,
So he must sip and think
Of better drink
He may attain to, after he is dead.[38]

John Donne, the great preacher and poet, Dean of St. Paul's from 1621 to 1631, was a very different character from George Herbert. He was sensual by temperament, tormented by his passions, and inclined to read all religion egocentrically and to express his response to it in terms which are sometimes blatantly theatrical, but he too holds that the proper use of the joys of this world requires constant mindfulness that better still are the delights of the world to come. In his "Litanie" are these lines:

When senses, which thy souldiers are,
Wee arme against thee, and they fight for sinne,
When want, sent but to tame, doth warre
And worke despaire a breach to enter in,
When plenty, Gods image, and seale
Makes us Idolatrous,
And love it, not him, whom it should reveale,

23

When wee are mov'd to seeme religious
Only to vent wit, Lord deliver us.
    . . . . .
    That learning, thine Ambassador,
From thine allegeance wee never tempt,
    That beauty, paradises flower
For physicke made, from poyson be exempt,
      That wit, borne apt high good to doe,
      By dwelling lazily
On Natures nothing, be not nothing too,
That our affections kill us not, nor dye,
Heare us, weake ecchoes, O thou eare, and cry.[39]

Both Donne and Herbert illustrate the belief, as common among Anglicans as among Catholics, that man's best creations are fit gifts for God. A poem or a piece of music, a witty sermon or an embroidered Communion cloth, might each serve as a proper offering. So Donne and Herbert and other Anglican poets were able to write love poems to God, keeping often many of the conventions and much of the sensuous diction and imagery of profane love poetry. The beauties of verse, like any other earthly beauty, might be welcome to God if sincerely offered to Him by the devout. Some lines from a sonnet of Herbert illustrate something of this:

My God, where is that ancient heat towards thee,
Wherewith whole showls of *Martyrs* once did burn,
Besides their other flames? Doth Poetry
Wear *Venus* Livery? only serve her turn?
Why are not *Sonnets* made of thee? and layes
    Upon thine Altar burnt? Cannot thy love
    Heighten a spirit to sound out thy praise

24

As well as any she? Cannot thy *Dove*
Out-strip their *Cupid* easily in flight?
Or, since thy wayes are deep, and still the same,
Will not a verse run smooth that bears thy name? [40]

Another passage bears on the same point. It is essentially
a love song, but a love song to Christ.

The wanton lover in a curious strain
     Can praise his fairest fair;
And with quaint metaphors her curled hair
     Curl o're again.
Thou art my lovelinesse, my life, my light,
     Beautie alone to me:
Thy bloudy death and undeserv'd, makes thee
     Pure red and white.

When all perfections as but one appeare,
     That those thy form doth show,
The very dust, where thou dost tread and go,
     Makes beauties here. [41]

The Bible itself gave proof that literary art was
proper for the service of religion. A passage from John
Donne may serve as an example of what was said repeatedly:

There are not so eloquent books in the world, as the Scriptures . . . Thy style of the Scriptures is a diligent, and an artifi-
cial style; and a great part thereof in a musical, in a metrical, in
a measured composition, in verse . . . So the Holy Ghost hath
spoken in those Instruments, whom he chose for the penning of
the Scriptures, and so he would in those whom he sends for the
preaching thereof: he would put in them a care of delivering
God['s] messages, with consideration, with meditation, with
preparation; and not barbarously, not suddenly, not occasionally,

not extemporarily, which might derogate from the dignity of so
great a service.[42]

Since God had allowed the Bible to be phrased with
artistic skill and in the most sacred of texts had permitted music of words and poetry, surely man might
use his best literary talents when he wrote on divine
themes.

A "middle attitude," rejecting the too expansively
sensuous or even sensual quality of much Catholic art
and avoiding also the extreme Protestant distrust of all
that appeals to the senses, is the sign manual of the
great Anglican religious literature of the seventeenth
century. Sense images abound, the language is splendid
in its sensuous evocation, but there is, in contrast to
much Catholic literature, usually a pattern of restraint
and a recurrent emphasis on the idea that beauty of
words and images only typify or represent the ideal of
what is holy. They are not holy in themselves; they
are simply means of communicating the believer's response to holiness or ways of putting readers in a frame
of mind responsive to the central truths which are apart
from and above the world of material sense. The problem for the Anglican artist in words was to find the
object of sense which could typify and somehow make
the divine comprehensible to man. Herbert's poem
"The Windows" reveals much:

> Lord, how can man preach thy eternall word?
>   He is a brittle crazie glasse:
> Yet in thy temple thou dost him afford

> This glorious and transcendent place,
> To be a window, through thy grace.
>
> But when thou dost anneal in glasse thy storie,
> Making thy life to shine within
> The holy Preachers; then the light and glorie
> More rev'rend grows, & more doth win:
> Which else shows watrish, bleak, & thin.
>
> Doctrine and life, colours and light, in one
> When they combine and mingle, bring
> A strong regard and aw: but speech alone
> Doth vanish like a flaring thing,
> And in the eare, not conscience ring.[43]

The point is that just as color and light are blended by the church window, so in the truly good preacher there are blended sound doctrine and holiness of life. The appeal of the poem is to the eye as well as to the ear; the image of the window carries the idea; but the poem is not a celebration of the sanctity or necessity of stained-glass windows but of goodness of life and doctrine. The image appeals sensuously; it is simple, but ingeniously used, and we are perhaps readier to accept Herbert's preaching because he has made it agreeable. Altars, vestments, incense, flowers, birds, brooks, trees, melting snowdrifts — anything in the whole order of creation — might supply images for Anglican poetry or prose, but the emphasis was put on a doctrine or a truth, a moral dogma or a holy emotion, not on the material object itself.

The great Anglican religious artists of the seventeenth century got their effects not only from their images but from a wide range of other rhetorical devices. "Wit" in the sense of ingenuity of thought and phrase was one; another was the skillful use of strongly marked rhythms and of sheer musical effects in prose. Jeremy Taylor was — and is — famous for his luxuriously developed similes; Donne excelled in the imaginative vision with which he chose images freighted with intellectual and emotional suggestion and also in his talent for building suspense and climax by the sound and movement of his style as well as by the sense of the words out of which he built his architectonic paragraphs. And a whole group of Anglicans wrote religious poetry rarely equaled since in English by using essentially the same rhetorical means as the prose writers and expressing in their stanzas the same emotional vigor and the same power in fusing content and form.

All this — the whole harvest of a "golden age" of religious writing — was accessible to English Puritans and their brethren on these shores, but little of it — Herbert's poems seem to have been exceptions — was much read in New England, and still less of it seems to have directly influenced what Puritans here or in England wrote. It was not that the more extreme Protestants rejected all that the Anglicans considered good in style or that they were wholly blind to the artistic virtues of Anglican poetry and prose, but simply that for their purposes and to suit their intellectual and moral scheme they preferred a way of writing determined by a different conception of the function of rhetoric. They had no aversion to similes and metaphors, or to symbolism and imagery as such; they too wrote with "wit" and used musical effects in prose as well as verse. On occasion they produced paragraphs or even pages which use precisely the same methods and material as the Anglicans, and are as impressive and as moving as the best of Lancelot Andrews, Herbert, Jeremy Taylor, or Donne. But ordinarily their work shows unmistakable differences from that of their colleagues in the established church; not, it seems, because it is less carefully wrought or less securely grounded in rhetorical principle, but because it was written by men who distrusted everything Catholic and most things Anglican and thought that there were artistic traditions and rhetorical schemes which were more authoritatively sanctioned than those in vogue among the court divines of London or the writers of Rome. The Puritan obviously wanted to choose the literary rule which seemed to him best justified morally and intellectually and, in its adaptation to its audience, most useful for the immediate purposes of zealous Protestant reformers and champions of a "purer" way of faith and life. He needed fit means to communicate and, if possible, to give lasting expression to his exalted sense that holy living was the one adventure worthy of the full energies of strong and determined men. Only a carefully thought out literary theory could be equal to the task. In his effort to find and follow one the Puritan met problems, as every religious artist must whatever his creed. Those problems, the ways in which he tried to solve them, and some of his artistic achievements and shortcomings, are the themes of the chapters which follow.

II

THE PURITAN LITERARY ATTITUDE

THERE is nothing in the religious literature of Puritan New England to match the richest pages of the great seventeenth-century Anglicans. It is a far cry from the poems of Herbert and Vaughan to the verses of Anne Bradstreet and the jog-trot measures of Michael Wigglesworth's *Day of Doom*, or from the magnificence of Jeremy Taylor's prose or Donne's to the best that the colonists wrote. But this is not to say that that best had no merit. There are many flashes of poetry, many passages of eloquent prose, and, throughout, a style that rarely descends to mere tame mediocrity. The work of the best writers in colonial New England shows that they wanted to write well as one way of serving God, and reflects both their zeal and their concern for fundamental stylistic values.

The more this work is examined in the light of the handicaps the colonists faced and the standards they set for themselves, the more impressive it becomes. In seventy years they made Boston second only to London in the English-speaking world as a center for the publishing and marketing of books, and they produced a body of writing greater in quantity and quality than that of any other colonial community in modern history. Its merits may escape him who reads as he runs, but to the more patient it may offer fuller insight into the best qualities of the Puritan settlers and their eagerness to find an adequate literary creed for pious purposes. The study of it may encourage a valuable humility in the face of the problem of religious expression as it exists even in our own times.

It is important first of all to realize that the American Puritan who wanted to be an artist in words — or, to put it more explicitly, who wanted to communicate his thoughts and emotion to others in such a way as to convince and move them — was faced by certain tangible handicaps. He was a colonist, and New England, compared to London, a wilderness. George Herbert in his quiet Wiltshire parish, John Donne in the deanery of St. Paul's, or Jeremy Taylor in the calm retirement of the Golden Grove, enjoyed advantages .denied the pioneer Bostonian. They had within reach — at the most only a few days' journey away — the best libraries and the best intellectual society of which England could boast. Their place as scholars and artists was recognized; they could count on readers and hearers able to appreciate fully not only the substance of what they wrote but whatever literary skill they showed in it. They might be mystics or rationalists, high-church men or liberals, Calvinists or Arminians, and there were enough like-minded readers to welcome them. They might use the classics or the church fathers, experiment with all the devices of rhetoric, and seek out new images for their ideas, secure in the knowledge that learned readers trained in an artistic tradition would acclaim their successes. But the New England colonist had no library to compare with those to be found in London; his audience, although eager, was limited in its tastes and inexperienced in literary niceties. If the colonial writer yearned for "good talk" or lively debates on literary problems he had to choose his companions from a very few, and some of those were sure to be separated from him by hours of travel on a difficult or dangerous road. He did read and he did write, but he could do so only as the exigencies of life in a pioneer community left him leisure. And even when Boston grew to a town of comfortable size and colonial life became relatively easy, the learned man and would-be artist was almost inevitably also a man whose political or religious duties engrossed much of his time. Anyone who can picture the hardships and practical complications they had to meet will be more inclined to wonder that Puritan writers wrote as much and as well as they did than to cavil at the fact that their work sometimes shows signs of crudity or haste.

No great artist, however, has ever been made or marred by the purely material conditions under which he worked. Geniuses have flourished in attics and mere scribblers in great libraries. The Puritan writer had many concrete obstacles to surmount, but his stylistic practice and his successes and failures were determined not so much by the fact that the ink sometimes froze in his inkwell as he worked, or by anything else in his environment, as by the ideas he held and those he rejected. These ideas, theological and philosophic, affected more profoundly than any material circumstance what he wrote and how.

To begin with, he was a Puritan — that is, an extreme Protestant. He found in Scripture no authority for vestments or "the painted texts" with which George Herbert thought the parson should adorn his church. From this the strict Puritan concluded that such things were improper, since God would have asked for them had he wished them. The fact that Catholics and high-church Anglicans alike used incense, organ music, and other means of sensuous appeal in worship was, for the Puritan, proof of their sinful neglect of Scripture. So also in literature. Catholic writing as a whole was evil; so was such Anglican literature as seemed to him un-sound in doctrine. Therefore he not unreasonably linked his distrust of ideas that seemed to him unworthy of a good Protestant with a dislike for the style in which those ideas were most commonly set forth.

The dislike is easy to illustrate. John Cotton, for example, while he was an Anglican at Cambridge Uni-versity, was famous for brilliant sermons, "elegantly and oratoriously performed," and was "applauded by all the gallant scholars," but when he became a Puritan he chose instead to preach in a "plain, honest" style.[1] One of his Puritan biographers praises him for giving up the "florid strains" which "extremely recommended him unto *the most*, who relished the *wisdom of words* above the *words of wisdom*" and admired "pompous eloquence." [2] Thomas Hooker of New England is clearly referring to the Anglican preachers of the early

34

seventeenth century when he says, "I have sometime admired . . . why a company of Gentlemen, Yeomen, and poore women, that are scarcely able to know their A.B.C. . . . have a Minister to speake Latine, Greeke, and Hebrew, and to use the Fathers, when it is certaine, they know nothing at all." The result is, Hooker thinks, that they "goe to hell hood-winckt, never awakened." [3] Richard Mather, another pioneer New England minister, "studiously avoided obscure phrases, Exotick Words, or an unnecessary citation of Latine Sentences, which some men addict themselves to the use of . . . This humble man" looked "upon the affectation of such things . . . to savour of Carnal wisdome." [4] Still another New Englander, Ebenezer Turell, writing in the eighteenth century but echoing an old refrain, says that a minister gives offense if he uses "the Jargon of Logic and Metaphysicks" or amuses his audience with foreign names "or soars above them in Flights of Poetry and Flourishes of rhetorick." [5] The references in such passages as these are clearly to common features of the style of many Anglican sermons.

All this is related, of course, to the difference between the Catholic and Protestant attitudes on the use of sensuous material in religious literature. The settlers of Massachusetts Bay found little room in their scheme of things for the graphic arts, or for any art which seemed only to please the senses. As Perry Miller puts it:

The Puritan lived in this world, and tried desperately not to be of it; he followed his calling, plowed his land, laid away his shillings, and endeavored to keep his mind on the future life. He looked upon the physical world as the handiwork of God, and the charms of the universe as His creations, and yet he told himself, "Get thy heart more and more weaned from the Creature, the Creature is empty, its not able to satisfie thee fully, nor make thee happy." [6]

The beauties of the physical world were all too likely to distract men's minds from religious truth or to arouse in them feelings alien to those proper for the study and worship of the divine. The Anglican John Donne wrote in a famous passage describing his preaching,

I am here speaking to you . . . you are here now, hearing me, and yet you are thinking that you have heard a better sermon somewhere else, of this text before; you are here, and yet you think you could have heard some other doctrine . . . delivered somewhere else with more edification to you; you are here, and you remember yourselves that now ye think of it: this had been the fittest time, now, when everybody else is at church, to have made such and such a private visit; and because you would be there, you are there. [7]

And in another sermon Donne said:

There are many comings to church; comings for company, for observation, for music; and all these indispositions are ill at prayers; there they are unwholesome . . . He that brings any collateral respect . . . to a sermon, loses the blessing of God's ordinance in that sermon: he hears but the logic, or the rhetoric, or the ethic, or the poetry of the sermon, but the sermon of the sermon he hears not. [8]

Anglicans and Puritans agreed about the ease with which in worship, prayer, or religious contemplation men's minds might wander away from the spiritual. Where Donne and most English churchmen differed from most Puritans was in the methods by which they tried to hold men's attention. To judge from their practice, the Anglicans and Catholics believed that one reason for using wit and rhetoric and imagery and material which catered to the senses as well as to the intellect in religious writing was that such things served to control the reader's unruly mind. But the Puritan made fewer concessions to human frailty, perhaps because he was more convinced of how frail man is. He kept away from anything, however appealing, that he thought might make men's hearts stray from theological truth and self-forgetful devotion toward pleasantly sensuous reveries on this world.

Obviously some types of imagery would be frowned on by the Puritan. He did not like the use of concrete material symbols in worship; he objected to the sign of the cross in baptism. In writing, therefore, he was not likely to rely on such things for his effects, and such sensuous material as he used was not drawn from the trappings of Catholic and high-church ritual. George Herbert's "The Windows," in its use of the symbol of the stained-glass window as a way of making a valid point about the preacher's need to combine with good doctrine a good life, was not a poem which would please the stricter Protestants. When Puritans thought of colored windows it was not with pleasure. "Painted obscure Sermons (like the painted glass in the windows that keeps out of the Light) are too oft the markes of painted Hypocrites." "The paint upon the glasse may feed the fancy, but the room is not well lighted by it." [9]

Nor would a radical New England Puritan like John Endicott, who cut out the cross from the English flag, have relished Donne's poem on the cross. In it Donne wrote:

> Who can deny mee power, and liberty
> To stretch mine armes, and mine owne Crosse to be?
> Swimme, and at every stroake, thou art thy Crosse;
> The Mast and yard make one, where seas do tosse,[10]

and then proceeded to play on the possibilities of the cross as a symbol in nature and on "cross" as a word of many meanings. To most Puritans this would have been at best idle fooling; at worst, sinful centering on the material at the expense of the spiritual. Anything that seemed to them to amuse or to delight sensuously or intellectually, at the expense of total concentration on theological truth and proper devotional feeling, was to be avoided in writing no less than in worship. This meant, since fallen man's passions were what they were, that much material ordinarily useful in literature was by the Puritan used very warily or not used at all. It would be useless to hunt for a Puritan poet who could write, as the Catholic Crashaw did, of the wounds on Christ's feet as mouths with full-bloomed lips, to be kissed with rapture. The Puritan would say that such imagery would so stir the sensual in man as to blind him to anything spiritual in the poem. The same theory, applied even to more innocent material, narrowed greatly the resources of the Puritan artist when he wrote on pious themes.

Another problem which the Puritan faced when he

set himself to write on "divinity" was common to all religious writers and particularly acute for the extreme Protestant, who in Calvinistic fashion exalted God and minimized man. This was the feeling that to go too far in trying to define or to explain religious mysteries or God himself was impious and dangerous, since it might easily result in men's making God nothing but an image of themselves, "a *Baby-god* . . . which like little children, they have dressed up out of the clouts of their own fond Phancies." "Words and syllables which are but dead things, cannot possibly convey the living notions of heavenly truths to us. The secret mysteries of a Divine Life, of a New Nature, of Christ formed in our hearts; they cannot be written or spoken, language and expressions cannot reach them." [11] The man who wrote this was an Anglican, but one whom the Puritans reverenced, and the quoted sentences come from a sermon preached before the Puritan House of Commons in 1647. Sir Thomas Browne, no Puritan, but a liberal churchman, touched epigrammatically on the same idea when he asked, "Who can speak of Eternity without solœcism?" [12] And a classic statement on the same theme is in Richard Hooker's great defense of Anglicanism:

Dangerous it were for the feeble brain of man to wade far into the doings of the most High; whom although to know be life, and joy to make mention of his name; yet our soundest knowledge is, to know that we know him not as indeed he is, neither can know him: and our safest eloquence concerning him, is our silence . . . He is above, and we upon earth; therefore it behoveth our words to be wary and few.[13]

39

The Puritan held that God was entirely beyond man's comprehension and could "never be delineated even momentarily in any shape, contour, or feature recognizable to human discourse." [14] As John Preston, an English Puritan, phrased it, "The vale of mortality doth hide us, it covers *God* from use . . . As a weake eye is not able to behold the Sunne . . . no more can you see God in his Essence." [15]

Here, surely, was a dilemma for the religious writer. If he was to speak of God at all he must somehow do so in finite and comprehensible words, and yet by definition God was incomprehensible and not to "be delineated even momentarily" in "human discourse." Hence came the general Protestant tendency to deplore "that tone of familiarity which is so distressing in so many devotions used by Romanists." [16] The idea that words about God should be "wary and few," and that theoretically at least the "safest eloquence concerning Him is . . . silence," made for a certain reticence among moderate Anglicans and Puritans, and led them often to sheer away from such passionate outbursts as Crashaw's poem on Christ's wounds.

The same reticence was encouraged by the general dislike felt by all the orthodox Protestants, Puritans or not, for the so-called "enthusiasts." These, appearing in a variety of sects in England in the seventeenth century, "thought themselves inspired with a Divine spirit" and believed that they enjoyed a direct and intimate relation with God.[17] So believing, they might, of course, write of their intimacy with the divine in terms shocking to more staid Protestants who were sure that God was unknowable in finite terms. In New England Anne Hutchinson and the Antinomians were regarded as "enthusiasts" and soon after Massachusetts Bay was founded they became thorns in the side of the Puritan clergy. They seemed a menace to the whole structure of the Puritan church and state, and the harshness with which they were treated reflects the intensity of the animosity they provoked. England, too, had its troubles with "enthusiasts" denouncing learning and formal theology, rebelling against the established forms in church, state, and society, and offending the Puritan, who was sure that the Bible contained all of God's law, as well as the Anglican, who reverenced also the traditional authority of a church.

In seventeenth-century religious literature in both Englands there is, therefore, often a tone of caution, a dread of "enthusiasm," which is reflected especially in vocabulary.

Consciousness of the fires of passion smouldering under the thin pall of decorum . . . made men strengthen all the reserves of self-control . . . This is one reason why the romantic amateur of the intensities of human nature is likely to be a little disappointed in much of the literature of this period. Excess of passion was too present a danger to tempt man to artistic exploitation.

Diction tended to restraint:

Certain words occur again and again. *Sober* is one of them . . . The Primate of Ireland . . . used three adjectives as tests for all thoughts, words, and actions. They were: *sober, just, godly.*

Comfortable . . . in the sense of giving comfort and assurance, is another . . . So is *sweet*, and *profitable* . . . These are all perfectly good words, expressive enough, but there is nothing very exciting in their aura of suggestion.[18]

For religious literature, at least in Puritan eyes, a vocabulary that was not very exciting had much to recommend it, since it could not smack of "enthusiasm" and was not likely to stir up men's senses to insurrection.

Still another determining influence on the Puritan artist was his reverence for the Bible. Theologically, of course, he depended on it as the one absolute authority, and in polity and doctrine followed it, or believed he did, to the letter. Inevitably, then, when he preached or wrote on divine themes he tended to limit his diction, his images, and his literary devices to those which he could find in Holy Writ. In subject matter too, obviously what was closest to the Bible was best. Biblical style was perfect because it was "penned by the Holy Ghost." It was a style of "great simplicitie and wonderful plainnesse," "unpolished," avoiding "the flowers of Rhetoricke," "the goodly ornaments of humane eloquence," and "wittie sharpe conceits." "If the Lord had penned yᵉ scriptures in such an eloquent stile as would have ravished the readers with delight, we would like fooles have stood admiring at yᵉ curious work of the casket, and never opened it to look upon the precious jewel therein contained; and have bin so much affected with the words, that in the meane time we would have neglected the matter." [19] The Puritan's rigid adherence to the literal word of God, as he understood it, would have been almost enough in itself to explain his avoidance of some material commonly used by Catholic and Anglican writers and to account for many of the standards he set for himself both in content and in style.

The most immediate influence on the Puritan's literary practice, however, especially in New England, was almost certainly the character of his audience. Whatever his theories might have been, it would have been hopeless for him to try to act on them if the result would not have won him readers and made them understand. By and large, the strength of Puritanism, here and in the mother country, lay in the plain man, eager for knowledge, better educated than his father had been, excited by the possibilities that books seemed to hold, but still unversed in literature as such and unable to grasp either the intricate rhetoric of learned and witty sermons like those of Lancelot Andrews, or the Latin and Greek quotations, the allusions, and the complicated imagery of much of the great Anglican religious literature of his time. Especially in preaching, a tradition had been built up for just such men — a tradition in which "plainnesse" was a literary virtue. Homeliness of imagery, simplicity of diction, and a constant emphasis on the values most easily recognizable by honest Englishmen of no pretensions to critical acumen characterized this style, and the influence of the audience in shaping it is patent. John Downame, an English Puritan, already quoted on the "simplicitie" and "plainnesse" of the Bible, wrote in the same passage that Holy Writ

was adapted "to the capacitie of the most unlearned." [20]
The Scriptures, he continued, "speak in the same manner, and injoyne the like obedience, to prince and
people, rich and poore, learned and unlearned, without any difference or respect of person . . . and therefore . . . the Lord . . . useth a simple easie stile fit
for the capacitie of all, because it was for the use of
all." [21]

The Puritan in New England did not believe in
political democracy, but he did believe that religious
teaching was a matter for all men, and he deliberately
directed most of what he wrote at the whole community.
Since most of his fellow colonists were relatively untutored it was clear that his style must be direct and
simple enough to strike home to them. There was always St. Paul's reminder, "Except ye utter by the
tongue words easy to be understood, how shall it be
known what is spoken?" [22]

Scattered everywhere throughout Puritan literature,
American and English, are reiterations of the idea that
the tastes and aptitudes of simple people must be catered
to in religious writing. Richard Baxter once wrote to an
Anglican friend, "Had I never been a Pastor nor lived
out of a College (and had met with such a taking
orator) I might have thought as you do. And had you
converst with as many country people as I have done,
and such country-people, I think you would have
thought as I do." [23] Clearly Baxter was linking
"country-people" and their religious needs with Puritanism, and associating Anglicanism with the learned in

colleges and those who had not "converst" with humbler folk. He seems to have been right; the extreme Puritanism of his day found its readiest audience among men who pretended to no social or intellectual eminence. Baxter's own poems, he thought, might "profit two sorts, women and vulgar christians and persons in passion and affliction." [24] He knew they would not please the wits, but as a good Puritan he was content to let them go out to help those who were unschooled in poetry but zealous in piety. Richard Mather in the colonies tried in his sermons to avoid certain tricks of style which, he thought, were useless and improper "in a *Popular Auditory*." [25]

For a variety of reasons, then, no colonial Puritan was likely to write as the Anglicans did, or to admit to his work some of the elements that gave special character to theirs. Not only did he have to contend with the conditions of life in a newly settled community, but his very Puritanism stood in the way of his accepting the aims and methods of, say, Crashaw and Donne. He suspected the "forms of art . . . identified with . . . forms of belief which" he thought false; [26] he was imbued with the Protestant distrust of the sensuous in devotion and worship; he was awe-struck by the incomprehensibility and inexpressibility of God; he was limited by his too literal reverence for the Bible; and he had always to shape his work to suit the literary capacities of a popular audience. The omens were not auspicious for art of the Anglican or Catholic variety, but the Puritan nonetheless produced a great deal of writing which, at its best, rises to a special dignity, shaped by the essential seriousness of his view of human and divine existence.

In meeting his artistic problem he had not only a few special handicaps but, mercifully, some sources of aid closely related to them. Colonial conditions, for example, were less easy for the artist than the atmosphere of literary London, but there were compensations. The colonists were eager for books. As zealous Puritans they believed learning was next to godliness and hardly to be separated from it. So schools, a college, printing offices, and bookshops came to New England — all aids in their way to the writer; and whatever difficulties he faced he knew at least that if he wrote the truth in terms that his audience could understand he could count on their response.

There is an ancient heresy to the effect that the Puritan was "hostile" to art and that one form of this hostility was an indifference to all matters of literary style. Actually, although there is in Puritan literature little formal literary criticism, and little discussion of the aesthetic aspects of writing, there are many passages which show that the Puritan thought long and hard about the problems of prose style and tried consciously to discover for himself a system of rules for giving adequate expression to his ideas and beliefs. It is interesting and touching to see how often Puritans, when explaining why and how they wrote as they did, confess their own shortcomings as artists, judged by the conventional standards of the literary elite. Even when they denounce the witty and overelaborate prose of their Catholic and Anglican contemporaries, there is sometimes a strong suggestion that they had more liking than they dared to confess, or their principles allowed them to indulge, for the literary flights which they professed to scorn. Downame, for example, seems to be "protesting too much" when he writes: "The flowers of Rhetoricke and helpe of wittie Sophistrie, is more fit for *Tullies* orations, whereby oft times a good cause is made bad, & a bad one good, right wrong, and wrong right, than for God's divine truth." [27] The Puritan was certainly well informed as to what the rhetorical principles and practices of his day were, and he must have understood that if his own work was to compete with that of the writers with whom he differed in creed or polity his style must be as carefully formed and as soundly grounded in rhetoric as theirs. He was able to convince himself, however, that if what he wrote was logically well ordered and rationally sound it would carry conviction, and he repeated again and again that if what he wrote was true and holy it needed no aid from mere literary ornamentation. Richard Baxter, looking back on his career as a preacher and writer, wrote lines that tell much of the Puritan literary attitude:

When I first intended *Writing* . . . being of their mind that thought that nothing should be made publike, but what a man had first laid out his choicest art upon; I thought to have acquainted the world with nothing but what was the work of *Time* and *Diligence*: But my conscience soon told me, that there was too much

47

of Pride and Selfishness in this; and that *Humility* and *Self-denyal* required me to lay by the affectation of that stile, and spare that industrie, which tended but to advance my name with men . . . The *Truths of God* do perform their work more by *their Divine Authority,* and *proper Evidence,* and *material Excellency* than by any *ornaments of fleshy wisdom:* and (as *Seneca* saith) though I will not despise an elegant *Physicion,* yet will I not think myself much the happyer, for his adding eloquence to his healing art.[28]

For Baxter, as for all good Puritans, the aim of good writing was to be useful; time spent on decoration or empty eloquence was time wasted; to waste time that might be devoted to God's service was, in the eyes of a Puritan, to sin. But although the Puritan was scornful of those who squandered precious hours merely to get literary reputation, he did insist on definite stylistic values. Of course "the Truths of God" did their work by their "Divine Authority," but their efficacy could be aided by the writer who gave them all possible clarity and stated them as directly and as plainly as he could.

Whatever the Puritan sacrificed artistically by his dislike for some of the material and manner of Anglican and Catholic literature, he made up for in part by the seriousness with which he concentrated on his effort to write clearly, logically, and simply. Moreover, his work often shows a positive conception of beauty. He believed that God had created an orderly and harmonious world, and held that in prose or verse, beauty came from harmony and order in the logical and reasoned statement of truth. Many Puritan writers in Massachusetts and in England wrote prose that is so lucid in its exposition and so firm in its structure that it became a powerful idiom not only for the Puritan but for hosts of men of other faiths who carried on the tradition after him.

The Puritans of course knew that no meaning can be conveyed except by something with which the senses can deal and therefore did not try to write without taking them into account. Where their special attitudes appear most plainly is in the character of the images they chose and in the way in which they elected to use figures. The method was dictated by the purpose. If a simile or metaphor made truth more intelligible and rationally more convincing it was good; if it simply tickled the senses and gave pleasure, or if it distracted the reader's attention from the doctrine, it was clearly bad.

William Perkins of Christ's College, Cambridge, who had a profound influence on New England thought in the days of the Puritans, wrote that "the Minister may, yea and must privately, use at his libertie the arts, Philosophy, and variety of reading, whilest he is in framing his sermon: but he ought in publike to conceale all these from the people." [29] The Puritans knew the difference between "studied plainness, and negligent rudeness"; [30] they knew that only by some calculated technique could they reach men's hearts, which were often approachable only through the fancy. Richard Sibbes, another English Puritan much read in New England, praised one of his colleagues because he "studied by lively representations to help men's faith by the fancy." After all, had not Christ taught by expressing "heavenly things in an earthly manner," and had not Solomon labored "to find out pleasant words, or words of delight"? [31] William Ames thought that the teacher "should not say that in two words which may be said in one; and that that key is to be chosen which doth open best, although it be of wood, if there be not a golden key of the same efficacy." [32] The use of the metaphor of the wooden and the golden keys certainly involves using two words where one might do, but the Puritan, whatever his emphasis on plainness in prose, knew that the fight was lost if he was plain to the point of being dull. He used figures of speech to explain and to illustrate the truth; he used them also because he knew that, whatever the ideal potency of divine truth might be, fallen man responded most directly to it when some concessions were made to his errant fancy. Constantly one feels in Puritan literature a conflict between the desire to convince and persuade by the readiest means, and the determination never to cross the line into pleasing the sensual man in such a way as to enslave even momentarily the spirit to the flesh.

Richard Baxter discussed more than once the proper attitude toward the senses. He seems to have been aesthetically more sensitive than some of his colleagues in the Puritan ministry and "thought that a painter, a musician, and a poet, are contemptible, if they be not excellent." He admits: "Harmony and melody are the pleasure and elevation of my soul," and adds a touching reminiscence of his wedded life: "It was not the least comfort that I had in the converse of my late dear wife, that our first in the morning, and last in bed at night, was a Psalm of Praise (till the hearing of others interrupted it)." [33] He found in "Holy Poetry" "somewhat of Heaven," because it charmed "souls into loving harmony and concord." [34] But even though he may have been especially inclined by temperament to appreciate the sensuous, it remains true that he was respected by Puritans here and abroad and that his theological and ecclesiastical views were generally accepted as orthodox. Naturally, as a writer, a lover of music, and a believer in excellence in art, and as an ardent servant of the Puritan faith, he had to ponder the place of the senses in holy living. His comments are not always explicit, but they are highly suggestive.

In common with most Puritans, he insists that the real power of a piece of writing comes from the truth it contains and the divine efficacy of that truth:

> Christ's living streams are the true Helicon:
> None make true poets but Heav'n's springs alone:
> What poor, low, toyish work make frothy wits!
> Like Bacchus' scholars in their pot-wise fits.
> Like children's poppets dress'd with lace and pin;
> Like handsome pictures; something wants within:
> A painted feast, carved with a painted knife.
> A living soul can feel it wanteth life. [35]

But even though to be "excellent," writing must stem from "Heav'n's springs," and although wit without the life of holiness could result only in "poor, low, toyish work," it seemed to Baxter that both the passions and the senses might play a useful part in "Holy Poetry." Of his own verses he said:

> They were mostly written in various passions . . . I confess that passion is oft such a hindrance of judgment, that a man should be very suspicious of himself till it be laid. But I am assured that God made it not in vain; and that reason is a sleepy half-useless thing, till some passion excite it. . . I confess, when God awakeneth in me those passions which I account rational and holy, I am . . . far from condemning them . . . Lay by all the passionate part of love and joy, and it will be hard to have any pleasant thoughts of Heaven.[36]

The crux here is, of course, the distinction between "rational and holy" passions which are good and others which are not. Baxter continues:

> I am an adversary to their philosophy that vilify sense . . . Human souls are not less sensitive for being rational, but are eminently sensitive. Yea, reason hath in it more of eminent internal sensation, than those men think that debase sense. The Scripture that saith of God, that he is life and light, saith also, that he is love, and love is complacence, and complacence is joy; and to say God is infinite, essential love and joy, is a better notion than . . . to say that God, and angels, and spirits, are but a thought, or an idea. What is Heaven to us, if there be no love and joy?[37]

This attack on the Stoics is a clear assertion that the senses are supposed to serve reason, but the love and joy Baxter has in mind is a love and joy centered on the divine.

A longer and clearer discussion comes in his *Saints Everlasting Rest*. There he admits that the senses are our "usual enemies" and the "usual means of drawing us from God," and he is careful to limit what he says to the "lawful delights of moderated senses." But "God would not have given us either our Senses themselves, or their usual objects, if they might not have been serviceable to his own Praise, and helps to raise us up to the apprehension of higher things." Therefore "it will be a point of our Spiritual Prudence . . . to call in our Sense" to assist faith. "If," Baxter continues, "we can make us friends of these usual enemies," the senses, "and make them instruments of raising us to God . . . we shall perform a very excellent work." The discussion is focused on the use of the senses as an aid in religious contemplation. Baxter recognizes that "bare Thinking" will not produce a "lively sense" of the divine. To achieve that is "the most difficult part of the work . . . its easier barely to think of *Heaven* a whole day, then to be lively and affectionate in *those thoughts* one quarter of an hour." "Sense hath its strength, according to the strength of the flesh: Faith goes against a world of resistance, but *Sense* doth not." [38]

What follows bears directly on the problem of the religious artist who wants to give his readers a "lively and affectionate" realization of the divine. "It is no easie matter," Baxter says, "to rejoyce at that which we never saw, nor never knew the man that did see it . . . But to rejoyce in that which we see and feel, in that which we have hold of . . . this is not difficult." "The holy Ghost doth condescend in the phrase of Scripture, in bringing things down to reach of Sense" and "sets forth the excellencies of Spiritual things, in words that are borrowed from the objects of Sense." "The new *Jerusalem*" is described "in expressions that might take even with flesh it self: As that the Streets and Buildings are pure Gold, that the Gates are Pearl, that a Throne doth stand in the midst of it . . . That we shall eat and drink with Christ at his Table in his Kingdom; that he will drink with us the fruit of the Vine." "These with most other descriptions of our glory are expressed, as if it were to the very flesh and sense." Such descriptions are, to be sure, "improper and figurative, yet . . . if such expressions had not been best, and to us necessary, the Holy Ghost would not have so frequently used them: He that will speak to mans understanding, must speak in mans language, and speak that which he is capable to conceive." [39]

Baxter's discussion, thus, while admitting the dangers of the senses, still recognizes their possible usefulness in helping men to faith and giving them a conviction of spiritual beauty. It is worth noticing, however, that he sticks closely to the Bible, and that he insists that sensuous terms are "improper" — that is, not completely fitting — for divine things. He warns, moreover, against letting sensuous imagery betray us into a false picture of heavenly reality. He asks, "Is it that we might think Heaven to be made of Gold and Pearl? or that we should Picture Christ, as the Papists do, in such a Shape? or that we should think Saints and Angels do indeed eat and drink?" and answers with an emphatic negative. But since we cannot conceive of Heaven or Christ or angels "in strict propriety," we must "conceive of them as we are able," and "the Spirit would not have represented them in these notions to us" if we had any "better notions to apprehend them by." Sensuous representations are "low notions" which should be used only as mirrors giving "exceeding imperfect" reflections. And Baxter then reiterates once more that phrases appealing to the senses are, in divine matters, "useful . . . but borrowed and improper." [40]

The task, then, of the pious man who would contemplate the divine in a "lively and affectionate" spirit is to keep in mind the perils of the sensuous, and the "impropriety" of sensuous images and words, but at the same time to "bring down" his "conceivings to the reach of sense." Unless we do that "we set God and Heaven so far from us, that our thoughts are strange, and we look at them as things beyond our reach, and beyond our line, and are ready to say, That which is above is nothing to us." Baxter is sure that we must never, "as the Papists, draw" holy things "in Pictures, nor use mysterious, significant Ceremonies to represent them" but we may none the less "get the liveliest Picture of them" in our minds that we can. "The familiar conceiving of the State of Blessedness, as the Spirit hath in a condescending language expressed it, and our strong raising of suppositions from our bodily senses, will further our Affections in" the "Heavenly Work" of contemplation. [41]

Baxter displays admirably the basic elements of Puritan thinking on the problem of religious art. Such theorizing as his opened the way for imagery and for sensuously appealing phrases, even though the Puritans still limited themselves by their conviction that only certain images and certain sensuous appeals could legitimately be used. They might be accused of making too free with God's majesty, and speaking too familiarly of themes on which, as Hooker said, our words should be "wary and few," but they could defend themselves by arguing, as Baxter did, that all they were doing was holding a glass up to the divine nature and that all that man could see was an imperfect reflection, not the eternal reality itself.

The Puritan was, as has already been pointed out, influenced as an artist, and in some respects limited, by his reverence for the letter of the Bible. Baxter's words show one way at least in which the Bible encouraged the Puritan to write more freely than he might otherwise have done. The Bible after all used men's language to appeal to men; it used parables, figures of speech, and allegory; it contained poetry and musical devices of style. There were references in it to many objects of sense. Plainly then, a Puritan was free to try his hand at parables, figures of speech, allegories, poetry, and prose harmonies. A book less rich as literature would have been a heavy clog on the Puritan religious artist, but in fact the Bible contained so much that was beautiful that it gave him considerable leeway in his own creative aspirations. His reliance on it for material and for method no doubt stifled his originality, but original or not, much of the soundest Puritan prose is moving in its diction and rhythm because the Scriptures had shown the way.

Finally, the fact that the New England Puritan had to direct what he wrote at an audience of plain men — sailors, fishermen, farmers, and small shopkeepers — although it made it impossible for him to write as he might have for a more expert literary clientele, called on him for special qualities of style. He knew that he must express his loftiest thinking in terms which would neither cheapen it nor leave it beyond the grasp of men who knew less about philosophy and abstract speculation than about the simple verities of the struggle for shelter, warmth, and food. Thence came the Puritan's love for homely realistic phrasing; for metaphors and similes not drawn from the classics or the world of books but from the common behavior of men and the common experiences of life; for a diction that was close to daily speech, and for figures that served to illustrate and explain rather than to ornament or to please the literary sophisticate. The Puritan concentrated upon the means by which he could clothe his ideas so as to awake his readers both to feel and to understand. He worked to find words and images and figures of speech to which his readers would immediately respond. He wanted to bring the "Mysteries of God" down to the "language and dialect" of simple people.[42] Baxter said that he tried "to speak and write in the keenest manner to the common, ignorant, and ungodly People (without which

keeness to them, no Sermon nor Book does much good)"
and therefore liked "to speak of every Subject just *as it
is*, and to call a Spade a Spade." [43]

But for the Puritan plainness in style did not imply
tameness. "The common vernacular, the English Bible
and the body of forms and images which had come
down" in popular preaching "from the medieval pulpit
supplied to the Puritan preachers an idiom by no means
barbarous, unaccustomed or lacking in vitality." [44] It
was an idiom in which "Similitudes" — metaphors or
similes — were commonly used "to win the hearer by
. . . plaine and evident demonstrations" and they were,
like the Biblical "Similies," taken from "persons, things,
and actions" which were "knowne, easie to be conceived,
and apt." [45]

"The word is like an exact picture, it looks every
man in the face that looks on it, if God speaks in it." [46]
"A wise man alwayes sailes by the same Compass,
though not alwayes by the same wind." [47] The homeliness of such sentences as these makes them the more
effective. They draw on the simplest material, but they
are vivid. Every reader of John Bunyan knows, of
course, that the dramatic power of *The Pilgrim's Progress,* or *The Life and Death of Mr. Badman,* comes
in large part from Bunyan's skill in colloquial diction
and his adroitness in using familiar material to symbolize or allegorize the divine. In his own apology for
his book, prefixed to *The Pilgrim's Progress* (which
was reprinted in Boston 1681 and 1706), he defends
"Types, Shadows, and Metaphors," pointing out that

the reader of the Bible is constantly dealing with symbols, allegories, and parables.

> Truth, although in Swadling-clouts, I find
> Informs the Judgement, rectifies the Mind;
> Pleases the Understanding, makes the Will
> Submit; the Memory too it doth fill
> With what doth our Imagination please.[48]

Bunyan and his fellow-Puritans knew that for a plain audience the "Swadling-clouts" of homely diction and imagery were better than the rich robes of elaborate rhetoric, allusion, and adornment with which Anglican preachers charmed the witty and learned. Everywhere in Puritan literature, here or abroad, there are characteristic images. Thomas Hooker says, "Take but an Apple, there is never a man under heaven can tell what tast it is of, whether sweet or soure, untill he have tasted of it; he seeth the colour and the quantity of it, but knoweth not the tast: so there is no man under heaven discerneth more of grace then he findeth in himselfe." [49]

Homeliness, of course, made for realism. The world of New England Puritan writers is one in which the sea, the forest, the field, and the village household appear vividly on every page, even those devoted to the most lofty points of doctrine. Here is another example from Hooker: "Sweep your hearts, and clense those roomes, clense every sinke, brush downe every cobweb, and make roome for Christ . . . And when thou hast swept every corner of thy house, doe not leave the dust behind the doore, for that is a sluts tricke: doe not remove sin

out of the tongue, and out of thy eye, and out of thy
hand, and leave it in thy heart." [50] John Cotton wrote:

And so an Huswife that takes her linning, she Sopes it, and
bedawbs it, and it may be defiles it with dung, so as it neither
looks nor smels wel, and when she hath done, she rubs it, and
buckes it, and wrings it, and in the end all this is but to make
it cleane and white; and truly so it is here, when as Tyrants
most of all insult over Gods people and scoure them and lay
them in Lee, or Dung, so as the very name of them stinks, yet
what is this but to purge them, and to make them white, and it
is a great service they doe to the people of God in so doing. [51]

Hooker writes of "Meditation":

Meditation is not a flourishing of a mans wit, but hath a set
bout at the search of the truth, beats his brain as wee use to say,
hammers out a buisiness, as the Gouldsmith with his mettal, he
beats it and beats it, turnes it on this side and then on that, fashions it on both that he might frame it to his mind . . . It's
one thing in our diet to take a snatch and away, another thing to
make a meal, and sit at it on purpose until wee have seen al set
before us and we have taken our fil of al, so we must not cast an
eye or glimpse at the truth by some sudden or fleighty apprehension, a snatch and away, but we must make a meal of musing.
[Meditation is] the traversing of a mans thoughts, the coasting
of the mind and imagination into every crevis and corner . . .
Meditation lifts up the latch and goes into each room, pries into
every corner of the house, and surveyes the composition and making of it, with all the blemishes in it. Look as the Searcher at the
Sea-Port, or Custom-house, or Ships . . . unlocks every Chest,
romages every corner, takes a light to discover the darkest passages . . . Meditation goes upon discovery, toucheth at every
coast, observes every creek, maps out the dayly course of a mans
conversation and disposition. [52]

The Puritan's earthy phrases and images, his restriction of his material to that supplied by the Bible or the everyday life of his audience, his seriousness of purpose, and his willingness to admit only those rhetorical devices and "similitudes" which served to drive home or to make more intelligible what he saw as the truth, were all directly related to his view of God and of man. The realism and concreteness of his work, the firmness of its structure, and its dignity of tone, all reflect the profound conviction from which it came.

He had a fundamental attitude toward life which formed and unified what he wrote. He concentrated theologically on predestination, on God's choice of the elect, and on the possibility of the elect's achieving some assurance of salvation. He saw this doctrine as one which accounted for much of what he found in life and as one which, properly interpreted, gave a motive for a constant striving for righteousness. Thence came a great concentration on the individual's walk with God. That was not a passive process; it was a struggle, worthy of a warrior. Life was for the Puritan an epic — an epic of ordinary men, who sought by fulfilling their part of a contract with God to achieve some assurance that God had chosen to save them. It was an epic that in its day and for Puritan men and women typified admirably the problem and the solution of living in this world, and Puritan literature, taken as a whole, is the expression of it. It had special validity for New England colonists, many of whom were actually warriors, seafarers, and pilgrims. It is easy to forget how moving

some of the conventional imagery of Puritan literature must have been to men who knew, or whose
fathers had known, what such words as "pilgrimage,"
or "wayfaring," or "the perils of the sea" really
meant.

No set of formulas can cover, of course, all that the
Puritans wrote, or explain the variety of their work,
the multiplicity of its themes, and the complications of
intellectual and theological history which it reflects.
But essential in most of it are its realism, its insistence
on solid content rather than superficial form, on rhetoric
as the servant of truth, and on "Words of Wisdom"
rather than the "Wisdom of Words." So is its habitual
dramatization of spiritual truth in terms of man's
struggle from darkness to light. Whatever subject is to
be discussed, the Puritan writer tries to make his argument or his exhortation strike home by putting it in
concrete terms that will ring true in the ears of an
audience of hard-working men.

Thomas Shepard believed that no one ever achieved
true holiness merely by studying books, and what he
wrote was: "*Jesus Christ* is not got with a wet finger." [53]
The image was vivid to his readers who, when they
read, patiently wet a finger to turn over the crowded
pages. Shepard knew, too, about "the peace that
passeth all understanding," and wanted his readers to
understand how it surpasses all joys on earth, but he
understood that the phrase might carry little force for
men to whom toil in this world was the everyday stuff
of experience. So he wrote:

Here's infinite, eternall, present sweetnesse, goodnesse, grace, glory, and mercy to be found in this God. Why post you from mountain to hill, why spend you your money, your *thoughts, time, endeavours,* on things that satisfie not? Here is thy resting place. Thy cloathes may warm thee, but they cannot feed thee; thy meat may feed thee, but cannot heal thee; thy Physick may heal thee, but cannot maintain thee; thy money may maintain thee, but cannot comfort thee when distresses of conscience and anguish of heart come upon thee. This God is joy in sadnesse, light in darknesse, life in death, Heaven in Hell. Here is all thine eye ever saw, thine heart ever desired, thy tongue ever asked, thy mind ever conceived. Here is all light in this Sun, and all water in this Sea, out of whom as out of a Crystall Fountain, thou shalt drink down all the refined sweetnesse of all creatures in heaven and earth for ever and ever. All the world is now seeking and tyring out themselves for rest; here only it can be found.[54]

In this passage, none of the dignity of the idea is lost, but the images — sweetness, clothes, money, meat, and physic; light, darkness, and the sun; fountains and the sea; and above all the sharp picture of a world tiring itself out in its search for rest — give life to the abstract idea because they are drawn freshly from experience and applied immediately to the individual. So far as any one paragraph can, this one illustrates the best qualities of Puritan prose. It shows the operation of a definite literary theory which, however much it might differ from those in vogue elsewhere, gave plenty of scope for an artist to write with imaginative force.

The theory was not of course invented by the Puritans. Ramus had taught them to think of rhetoric not as a system with rules of its own, separate from logic, but as one dependent upon it. Words corresponded to things; the art of style was fundamentally the arrangement of them in an order which agreed with the logical structure of the created universe and with the normal procedure of the mind in dealing systematically with ideas.[55] From the classics Puritan writers, like all well-educated men of their time, learned much about basic qualities of style even though they rejected the more complicated patterns and abstruse rhetorical doctrines of the ancients. When they read current English books they found a dazzling variety of styles. Richard Hooker's highly rhythmical and elaborately developed periods; the tricks of the Euphuists; the terseness of Bacon's apothegms and the lucid eloquence of his *Advancement of Learning*, with its comments on rhetoric; Robert Burton's intricate embroidery of allusions and quotations, which almost hid the plain texture of his own stylistic cloth; the so-called "metaphysical" prose and verse full of far-reaching metaphors, plays on words, sound echoes, hyperboles, and paradoxes, which were written by the great Anglican artists and even a few Puritans in the days of James I — all these literary modes were used in works which the Puritans could read. They might take as models, if they wished, anything from the extreme stylistic eccentricities of the Elizabethan and Jacobean wits to the deliberately limited diction and grave measures of the King James and Genevan Bibles. Their task was to choose what literary paths to follow, not necessarily to explore new ones.

Naturally they elected to take from the ancient and modern rhetoricians what seemed to them to consort with their philosophical and religious standards and to be best adapated for their special purposes. In so doing they achieved a stylistic synthesis, not radically original or new, since its elements were sanctioned by long usage and by reputable critical authority. It was their own, however, because their emphases, their preferences for particular literary types, and their selection among accepted rhetorical devices gave it a characteristic stamp, impressed upon it by fundamental Puritan attitudes toward letters. Their writing can be understood and criticized intelligently only when it is seen as the working out of a distinct literary theory more typical of them than of any other group. They formed and applied the theory in an attempt to answer the old riddle of how infinite and eternal verity is to be expressed in the finite terms comprehensible to mortal man. They did not always succeed but, as Shepard showed in his paragraph on the peace of God, their doctrine could be effective in the hands of the Puritan artist who wanted to drive home a "lively and affectionate" sense of the divine by shooting rhetorical arrows "not over his people's heads, but into their Hearts." [56]

III

PURITAN HISTORIANS:
"THE LORD'S REMEMBRANCERS"

THE devout New England colonist put his literary principles into practice in many kinds of writing. Puritan pulpit literature is, of course, the most voluminous record of his beliefs and contains much of his best prose, but his sermons have been more thoroughly studied than his other work and their subject matter is often relatively forbidding to modern readers.[1] It seems more profitable therefore, in a general study of the relation between some of the Puritan's theological doctrines and his literary strivings, to concentrate upon types of his writing which are no less revealing of his attitudes and skill, but better adapted to current tastes. Among such types his historical work is especially important. He took it very seriously and set a high standard for it. It preserves its interest both because it deals with an exciting chapter in the story of this country and because it displays some of the most important aspects of Puritan thought and life.

The sevententh-century man had a great reverence for history. For him it was "The Mistresse of Mans life," "Times witnesse, herald of Antiquitie, The light of Truth, and life of Memorie."[2] It was "a school of prudence"; it taught better than did the precepts of moral philosophy. Sir Thomas North thought histories were "fit for every place" and would "reach to all persons, serve for all tymes, teache the living, revive the dead, so farre excelling all other bookes, as it is better to see learning in noble mens lives, than to read it in Philosophers writings." [3] The classical historians were translated; Queen Elizabeth was a student of history; Sir Walter Raleigh thought it could triumph over time, and in 1614 brought out his own *History of the World*.[4] So marked was the "historical craze" that poets and defenders of poetry felt compelled either to challenge the historian's supremacy or to relate their work to his.[5]

Naturally, the English colonists in the New World, as men of the late Renaissance, thought highly of history. The more literate of them read widely in it, and just as they found in classic and modern authors a variety of accessible stylistic models, so in the historians they discovered different ways of interpreting and presenting the record of human affairs. The Puritans in New England liked especially the moralistic tone of some of the Greeks and Romans. In both Livy and Tacitus there were explicit statements of the ethical value of studying past events. Plutarch, of course, was primarily a teacher by means of biography and to Cotton Mather he seemed "incomparable." [6] Polybius praised history as "in the truest sense an education." [7] Cotton Mather thought that "a person of good sense" should know not only Polybius but Herodotus, Xenophon,

Diodorus Siculus, Dionysius of Halicarnassus, Suetonius, and Herodian, as well, of course, as Livy, Tacitus, and Plutarch.[8] Few colonists can have covered the whole list, but many of them certainly read enough samples from it to learn something of the matter and manner of the great chroniclers of the past.

If they preferred current books and current critics they found the familiar general dicta on the importance of history reinforced by scholarly arguments. Francis Bacon thought it was essential for the progress of learning and pressed the claims of "modern history." He also underlined the need to distinguish between "Memorials" — "first or rough draughts" — and "Just and Perfect History," by which he seems to have meant coherent and finished narratives which presented systematically selected and ordered material in decent literary form.[9] Bacon's concentration on statecraft and his somewhat Machiavellian point of view may have made some of his own historical writing unpalatable to the pious, but there is no question that in historiography as in other fields of scholarship his work and ideas were fertilizing influences.

"For the humanists of the Renaissance" and of Bacon's day, "history was philosophy teaching by examples"; [10] the Puritans agreed, and the more "moral" the philosophy the better the history. Moreover, as ardent Protestants they had a special interest in historical scholarship. For centuries earnest Christians had held a philosophy of history. The world proceeded according to divine plan. Even the story of the ages before Christ could be interpreted as the record of how the way was prepared for him. St. Augustine envisioned mankind as destined to go through pain and conflict to the eventual resolution of the Last Judgment, and Orosius wrote a history of the world which implemented this theory. Renaissance writers often linked history to religion by presenting it as a demonstration "of God working out His will in human . . . affairs," and "the conception of history as epic story and drama, not as scientific diagnosis, of individual men rather than social and economic forces as the causes of events" was often tied in with the notion that a prime value in any narrative of the past was its revelation of the power of holiness manifested in the triumphs of the righteous.[11]

This much was believed by most Christians when Virginia and Massachusetts were founded; fervent Protestants, especially the thoroughgoing Puritan reformers, went still farther in their reverence for history. It had for them, the direct heirs of the Reformation, a special meaning based on a tradition inherited from the first great pioneer rebels against Rome. "The Reformation . . . seems a strange starting-point for science yet it, even more than the Renaissance, brought out scientific methods of historical investigation."[12] Luther, Calvin, and the other Reformers tried to prove their case by historical evidence that their congregations and not the Catholic followed the original Christian pattern. They had to search out, collect, analyze, and criticize all the records of the Roman church; they had somehow to hold their own against its learned apologists.

A key book in the process was the so-called *Magde-burg Centuries* (1559–1574),[13] a huge annalistic source collection and commentary covering the first thirteen centuries of Christianity. It has been called "the first monument of modern historical research," [14] and even though its scientific quality may be challenged, and although on the literary side it had nothing to recommend it, it was a stimulus to the writing of religious and ecclesiastical history, an illustration of the propagandistic usefulness of such writing, and an example of research methods, and it influenced many later Protestant scholars and writers.[15] Some of the more learned Puritans in New England knew it at first hand; most of their fellow colonists who read or wrote at all had some contact with it through books which derived from it method, material, or both.

The most popular of such books was the famous Protestant "Book of Martyrs," John Foxe's *Acts and Monuments* (London, 1563). It owed much to the *Centuries,* as well as to Jean Crespin's *Livre des Martyrs* (1554). It became for many Puritans a devotional book second only to the Bible, and from it "the great mass of the people drew their knowledge of church history." It was for them the most popular, and therefore influential, treatment of the "heroic period of Protestantism." [16] Puritan children were encouraged to pore over its accounts of the fortitude of the martyrs. Scholars looked to it both for information and for pious tales with which to lighten a sermon or treatise or to point up an argument. Historians and biographers found in it a record of the lives of holy men, an interpretation of the four centuries before Wycliffe as the era of Antichrist, and a reading of all Christian history as a struggle between pure faith and Popery. Inevitably it became a useful guide for their own studies of the past.[17]

The Puritan historians, then, as sharers in a Protestant scholarly tradition, as readers of classical chroniclers who were also preceptors in ethics, and as students of contemporaneous translators and writers who coupled zeal for historical knowledge with a desire for aesthetic effect, had excellent sources of inspiration and excellent examples of method. In the colonies they had, moreover, special incentives to write, some of which are illustrated by an entry in the records of the Virginia Company.

On April 12, 1621, the "Court" of the Company greeted with "very great applause" a motion which read: "That for so much as ye lottaries were now suspended, which hetherto had continued the reall and substantiall food, by which Virginia hath been nourished . . . insteade thereof, shee might be now preserved, by divulginge fame and good report, as shee and her worthy Undertakers did well deserve." The Court felt, "that it could not but much advance the Plantation in the popular opinion of the Common Subjects, to have a faire & perspicuous history, compiled of that Country, from her first discovery to this day: And to have the memory and fame of many of her worthies though they be dead to live and be transmitted to all posterities." "The best now planted parts of America, under the Spanish government" by the time they were of the age of Virginia had "their Annales or histories," although they offered no "better matter of relation then Virginia." That colony, then, should have "a generall history (deduced to the life to this yeare)." Its effect "throughout the Kingdome with the generall and common Subject" could be gauged by the welcome given "little Pamphletts or declarations lately printed." But the history must be written soon, since a few more years "would . . . consume the lives of many whose livinge memories yet retayned much" and would destroy "those letters & intelligences which yet remaine in loose and neglected papers." [18]

The colonists knew that a real history of Virginia or Plymouth or Massachusetts might stir up the stay-at-home Englishman to throw in his lot with them by publishing their successes, by refuting misguided critics, and by giving prestige to the New World adventurers. The settlers were sure not only of the general utility of history but of the specific service it could be to them; they looked on historiography not as a luxury but as a central support for their enterprise.

The New England Puritans had, moreover, reason to believe that histories would be particularly valuable to them in their effort to set up in the wilderness a commonwealth of God. They were intellectually, politically, and economically less closely knit to the mother country than were most of their neighbors; they were dominated by men who were staunch adherents of a

73

religious polity unlike that of the Church of England or of English Presbyterianism. The scholars and teachers among them put learning next to godliness; historical learning was especially dear to them because they were sure it could be used to prove that their experiment in the colonies was a climactic phase of the steady advance of Protestantism since the Reformation. To write their own history seemed even more important to them than to the colonists elsewhere, because they were sure that the royalist and Anglican scholars in London would usually write it in unfavorable terms or, at the best, would overlook its full significance. That significance, the Puritans felt, must be realized if the colonists' own ardor was to be kept alive and if others of the godly and learned were to be enticed to join them. They felt that they were in special need of a defense directed as much to scholars as to workmen or merchants. Accordingly they believed that their appeal to the faithful in England would be strongest when buttressed by good histories.

They were disciples of a philosophy of history, soundly rooted in theology, which seemed to lend a special dignity to the story of their activities. God, they believed, directly manipulated human affairs, rewarding good men on earth and punishing bad, exerting his "providence" to uphold the good and crush the evil. Therefore, history might reveal what God approved or condemned; and when history showed that God had consistently favored an individual, a sect, or a nation, one must argue that he approved what he favored. What better proof of the righteousness of New Englanders could be found than historical evidence that they had been aided by "special providences," testimonies of God's affection for them? Given the right facts, a history could be made in effect a polemic for a creed.

The doctrine "that Providence intervened in the government of the world, and . . . that it was the business of the historian as a teacher of morality to point it out when he related the events," was held by others than Puritans — held, indeed, by "the Elizabethans in general." [19] Edmund Bolton, a Catholic, wrote just before Plymouth was settled that some ancient authors erred in that "the Part of heavenly Providence in the Actions of Men is generally left out . . . in their Histories." [20] Sir Walter Raleigh wrote his history mindful "that all the events . . . in the world were divinely ordained." [21] In history, he said, we see "how kings and kingdoms have flourished and fallen; and for what virtue and piety God made prosperous; and for what vice and deformity he made wretched, both the one and the other." And in a brief summary of parts of modern history Raleigh demonstrated "the bitter fruits of irreligious policy" and that "ill doing hath always been attended with ill success." [22] Far more than most of their contemporaries, however, the New England Puritans emphasized the idea that history was primarily a record of God's providences.

Historians with such a theory may succumb to temptation and suppress whatever fits in badly with it, thus

falsifying for the sake of a doctrine. But the Puritans'
wholehearted belief in "Providences" involved a confidence that, since all events were controlled by God,
all were worth recording as evidence of the divine will.
The historian, therefore, must so far as possible set
down everything, without imposing on the facts any
personal prejudice or individually contrived principle of
selection. This, in theory at least, blocked the way
toward history which was merely an arbitrary collection of data selected in order to prove a thesis in theology, and although the best New England historians
certainly violated the principle by choosing some of
their materials with an eye to literary effect or to polemic
or propagandistic exhortation, on the whole they tried
faithfully to give a complete and accurate record of
every event.[23]

Their concern for history bore good fruit. Since the
Puritan regarded historical writing as a labor important
in spreading religious truth and as a useful way of
carrying out God's will on earth, he dedicated himself
to it with enthusiasm, brought to his task as a historian all the skill he possessed and wrote as well as
he knew how. To the modern reader the histories
written by the colonists are generally speaking more
appealing than other colonial literature, not only in
content but in style. In them appear the best qualities
of Puritan writing — the characteristic seriousness and
dignity, the sound and orderly structure, and the "plain"
and realistic language. In them appear, too, the spirit
and temper that made the Puritan a successful colonist.

He conceived of the godly life as an epic — a pilgrimage from darkness to light, a warfare against odds, a spiritual voyage through all sorts of perils to an ultimate safe haven. Therefore he dramatized his own history. The migration to New England was for him not simply the movement of a group of English colonists to a new country in order to set up there a prosperous community of their own. There were overtones that altered the character of the bare fact. The Puritans liked to think of themselves as a new "chosen people," delivered from an England which had become for them an Egypt, led by God's power across the sea toward a New World which God would make for them a Canaan. They were not merely plain English folk, taking ship to cross the Atlantic, and, once on these shores, building towns and clearing woodland. They were an army — an army of Christ — fighting the newest engagement in the age-old war between God and Satan; they were a band of pilgrims steadfastly pushing on day by day toward a Holy Land; they were not only literally voyagers — they were spiritual seafarers venturing their lives to conquer new territories for God. They gave vitality and meaning to their adventure by conceiving of it in terms of a splendid myth. They warmed with a sense of kinship to the Jews led out of Egypt; they were enthusiastic in their confidence that however obscure they might be in this world, they were in the eyes of God his champions and the leaders of the most recent advance of true Christianity. For them the Protestant Reformation seemed the dawn of a new day; they worked hard and long because they were sure that their adventure was a Reformation, too, and that they were winning new victories for Christ.

Much of their historical writing, of course, was merely a sober record of fact, but many pages are genuinely dramatic because they reflect the Puritan's vision, which translated that fact into a part of a great myth. The simplest items of experience could be glorified as proofs of the magnificence of God's work in manipulating the affairs of earth. The most commonplace event could be interpreted to fit the Puritans' symbolizing of themselves as heroic soldiers of Christ, conquerors in the service of God, and pilgrims moving steadily toward glory greater than this world's.

The earliest of the New England historians was William Bradford, and his "History of Plimouth Plantation" has become, deservedly, an American classic. Bradford was a Yorkshire yeoman, who came to Plymouth in 1620, and in 1621 was chosen governor of the colony. He held the governorship for most of the rest of his life, but in spite of the burdens of office, began to write his "History" in 1630 and worked on it for twenty years. He was not the man to waste time on a literary whim, or to take precious hours for writing without a practical aim. Yet his history was clearly planned as a book and obviously shaped to reach an audience — proof of his conviction that an accurate record of his colony would serve it usefully. Had he lived longer and had more leisure, he might have polished his work further and have found a publisher; as it was, his manuscript, although not printed until 1856, was known to some of his compatriots in the seventeenth century, and thus played a part in supplying material and establishing standards for other New England writers.

On the very first page he shows the Puritan's desire to tie his colonial adventure into a larger scheme of historical development. He writes:

> It is well knowne unto the godly and judicious, how ever since the first breaking out of the lighte of the gospell, in our Honourable Nation of England (which was the first of nations, whom the Lord adorned ther with, affter that grosse darkness of popery which had covered, and overspred the Christian worled) what warrs, and opposissions ever since Satan hath raised, maintained, and continued against the Sainots, from time to time, in one sorte or other.

Then follows a brief sketch of some of Satan's "wars and oppositions" from the time of the first Christians to Bradford's own, leading up to the emigration of the Pilgrims to Holland in 1607 and 1608.[24] Thus, in his first chapter, Bradford demonstrated that the facts he was to treat were significant not simply in themselves but as parts of an age-old struggle between God and the devil, and formed a special stage in Protestantism's triumphant progress. The title for the whole first section of his history is "Of Plimmoth Plantation. And first of the occasion and Indusments ther unto; the which that I may truly unfould, I must begine at the very roote and rise of the same" — further evidence of Bradford's desire to place his narrative in historical perspective.[25]

He shows, too, the Puritan conception of history as a record of God's providential management of the world. This, with other elements in his historical creed, is plainly stated in a passage at the end of his sixth chapter:

I have bene the larger in these things, and so shall crave leave in some like passages following, (thoug in other things I shal labour to be more contracte,) that their children may see with what difficulties their fathers wrastled in going throug these things in their first beginnings, and how God brougt them along notwithstanding all their weaknesses and infirmities. As allso that some use may be made hereof in after times by others in shuch like waightie imployments.[26]

Here Bradford confesses to a principle of selection, or at least of emphasis, based on his view of what history should be — a memorial to the pious, a testimony to God's providential power, and a useful lesson for present and future.

Bradford was not a trained craftsman, but he had a feeling for style, and the best passages in his work are splendid prose. He said that he was trying to write "a plaine stile; with a singuler regard unto the simple trueth in all things" — an admirably succinct phrasing of a cardinal tenet in Puritan literary theory.[27] But his plainness is not mere plainness; his enthusiasm for his theme, his sharp ear for earthy speech, his shrewdness in selecting homely images, and his eagerness to convey to his readers his own sense of the dramatic quality of the story he is telling, give distinction to most of his pages. Even when he is most hurried, and content with the barest chronological scheme, he rarely blurs his effects. He had an untutored sense for a good story, a knack for the orderly knotting-up of every thread he started to trace, and, as a special gift, rare among Puritan writers, a vein of humor.

One of his stylistic traits appears at the end of the fifth chapter, where he uses a moral aphorism for climax: "A right emblime, it may be, of the uncertine things of this world; that when men have toyld them selves for them, they vanish into smoke." [28] Similarly he accents an argument by the simple comment on his adversary's reasons, "Bad logick for a devine." [29] The moving simplicity of his narrative can be illustrated from almost any section of the book dealing with action, and his feeling for a homely story as a means of pointing a truth comes out in such passages as the one which compares certain unwelcome colonists to "the hedghogg whom the conny in a stormy day in pittie received" and "in the end with her sharp pricks forst the poore conny to forsake her owne borrow." [30] Bradford's phrasing is not that of the imaginative artist, wide-ranging in metaphor and simile, nor that of the scholar, ransacking books for illustrations and parallels, but that of the man whose ears were full of the plain speech of English farmers and who was bred to relish simple rhythms and words rich with the sense of familiar life. So he writes of "a very drunken beast" who "did nothing . . . but drink, and gusle, and consume away the time and his victails," or tells how Thomas Morton's house was "demolisht," "that it might be no longer a roost for shuch

unclaine birds to nestle in." On another occasion enemies of the colony, confused by the Governor's return,
"were somwaht blanke at it," but soon "as briske as
ever." [31] Here is his answer to the charge that New
England water was bad: "If they mean, not so wholsome as the good beere and wine in London, (which
they so dearly love,) we will not dispute with them;
but els, for water, it is as good as any in the world, (for
ought we knowe,) and it is wholsome enough to us that
can be contente therwith." [32] This has the tone that has
marked New England humor for generations; so does
Bradford's contemptuous retort to those who complained about mosquitoes, "we would wish shuch to
keepe at home till at least they be muskeeto proofe." [33]
The introduction of John Lyford, that "eminente person" whom Bradford so thoroughly disliked, is in the
same vein as Dickens's presentation of Uriah Heep:

When this man first came a shore, he saluted them with that
reverence and humilitie as is seldome to be seen, and indeed made
them ashamed, he so bowed and cringed unto them, and would
have kissed their hands if they would have suffered him; yea, he
wept and shed many tears, blessing God that had brought him
to see their faces; and admiring the things they had done in
their wants, etc. as if he had been made all of love, and the humblest person in the world. [34]

Irony is here keyed to accurate characterization. Bradford was not interested in rousing laughter for its own
sake, or for literary effect apart from its value in driv-
ing home essential historical fact, but he had a sure
instinct for the kind of style, seasoned with humor,

which might win a Plymouth audience. No other seventeenth-century American historian can be read today with so much pleasure, because in no other was the manner of expression so well adapted to bring out both the dramatic quality of the story and the author's conviction of its importance.

That conviction appears most clearly in the passages of exalted prose which occur where he is most moved. In them the style preserves its individuality, but at the same time owes much to typical Puritan stylistic theory and to the Puritan concept of history. An example is the description of the plight of the Pilgrims just after they landed:

> Being thus passed the vast ocean . . . they had now no freinds to wellcome them, nor inns to entertaine or refresh their weatherbeaten bodys, no houses or much less townes to repaire too, to seeke for succoure. It is recorded in scripture as a mercie to the apostle and his shipwraked company, that the barbarians shewed them no smale kindness in refreshing them, but these savage barbarians [the Indians] . . . were readier to fill their sides full of arrows then other wise. And for the season it was winter . . . For summer being done, all things stand upon them with a wetherbeaten face; and the whole countrie, full of woods and thickets, represented a wild and savage heiw. If they looked behind them, ther was the mighty ocean which they had passed, and was now as a maine barr and goulfe to seperate them from all the civill parts of the world . . . What could now sustaine them but the spirite of God and his grace? [35]

Bradford follows this, and brings his chapter to a climax, by making an appeal to succeeding generations to remember the settlers of Plymouth, and in characteris-

tic Puritan fashion, he turns to the words and rhythms
of the Bible.

May not and ought not the children of these fathers rightly
say:
*Our faithers were English men which came over this great ocean,
and were ready to perish in this willdernes, but they cried unto
the Lord, and he heard their voyce, and looked on their adver-
sitie . . . .Let them therfore praise the Lord, because he is good,
and his mercies endure for ever. Yea, let them which have been
redeemed of the Lord, shew how he hath delivered them from
the hand of the oppressour. When they wandered in the deserte
willdernes out of the way, and found no citie to dwell in, both
hungrie, and thirstie, their sowle was overwhelmed in them. Let
them confess before the Lord his loving kindness, and his won-
derfull works before the sons of men.*[36]

One more sentence must be quoted, because it sounds
the dominant theme of Bradford's book. He is writing
of the departure from Leyden: "So they lefte the
goodly and pleasante citie, which had been ther resting
place near 12 years; but they knew they were pilgrimes,
and looked not much on those things, but lift[ed] up
their eyes to the heavens, their dearest cuntrie, and
quieted their spirits." [37] The Puritans succeeded as pioneers and state-builders in large part because they kept
before their eyes a clear vision of themselves as "pilgrimes" toward "the heavens, their dearest cuntrie."
For them one great function of historical writing was
to symbolize concretely and dramatically that vision.

Bradford's was the first of a long series of histories
written by New Englanders in the seventeenth century.
No other English colony in the same period produced

so many works of the sort, a fact which strongly supports the conclusion that the Puritans had a compelling interest in historical writing and saw in it special value for their purposes. Some of the Puritan colonial histories, like William Hubbard's and Daniel Gookin's, tried to give the whole record of New England; others concentrated on special aspects of the story. Some were printed, some were not; they varied greatly in literary excellence and technical skill; but they all illustrate how important it seemed to pious New Englanders to set down the facts of their own history in order to protect themselves against the slanders of their enemies, and, more important still, in order to reveal how steadfastly God worked in the interests of his chosen people. By the end of the century there was awaiting publication in London Cotton Mather's *Magnalia Christi Americana*, a church history of New England, impressive in bulk and extraordinary for the mass of material it contains and for the literary skill of its best pages. It was printed in a large folio volume in 1702 and has been ever since a treasure house for all students of life and letters in colonial New England. A book on such a scale could not have been produced in Massachusetts if its author had not had the benefit of much historical work done earlier by other colonists, or if by the end of the seventeenth century there had not been in the Puritan colonies a mature sense of the value of history in a Bible commonwealth.

Earlier than Mather's opus, and the first general history of Massachusetts Bay to be printed, was a book by

Edward Johnson, which illustrates with special sharpness the close relation between Puritan theological doctrine and Puritan historical writing. It was published in London in 1653 as *A History of New-England*. Probably Johnson's own choice for a title was "The Wonder-Working Providence of Sion's Saviour in New England," and the page headlines carry this instead of the more general "History of New-England" which the publisher preferred for the title page. The longer name is admirably descriptive. The theme of the book was the "wonder-working Providence" which had made possible the colonists' success in a "howling desart." [38] In no other work is there such a vivid revelation of the early colonists' intense belief in God's partnership in their adventures; nowhere else is so clearly shown their full intellectual and emotional acceptance of the idea. What comes out of Johnson's pages is not exposition or preaching, forced upon a body of historical material, but the spontaneous expression of a man who saw history in terms of God's providence and found its meaning through his firm assurance that he and his compatriots were simply actors in a drama divinely written and staged. Johnson was not arguing a point; he was writing from an attitude central to his whole view of life. He sees the story of Massachusetts as an allegory, the splendid record of the armies of Christ triumphing over the Devil, thanks to the power of their leader. Allegory for Johnson was less a literary device than a natural form in which to express his burning confidence that he and his fellow-citizens were not only men but servants of Christ; not only pioneer settlers but leaders in a struggle of far more than earthly importance. New England survived and prospered because of God's benevolent providence; and the real story was not of the founding of towns or of Indian fighting but of the advance of Christ's forces against the wilderness and its pagans. Seen thus, it inevitably became an allegory, since the tale of events became a symbol for an action directed by God on a divine plane.

Essentially, then, Johnson clothed a central doctrine in his faith with the trappings of myth; he personified and dramatized a belief. On his theme and from his material a great artist might have written another *Holy War* or *Pilgrim's Progress*, but Johnson was not an artist but a woodworker, not even a preacher but a layman and man of affairs. When Woburn was incorporated in 1642 he became its leading citizen and for the better part of thirty years served as one of its selectmen. He was also its town clerk, captain of its military company, and its delegate to the colonial legislature. Between practicing his trade and living up to his official responsibilities, he can have had little time for writing. That his history came into being shows again how deeply rooted among Puritans was the idea that such books were necessary; that he wrote it largely in allegorical terms shows how common in New England was the tendency to interpret history as the limited and concrete dramatization of the play of supernatural forces. Had Johnson been a learned man, deeply versed in literature, his use of allegory might be seen merely as deference to a literary convention. As it is, it seems far more likely that he chose allegory simply because, so far as New England's history went, he thought of the acts of men and the purposes of God as two aspects of one story. History, as he saw it, could only be a record of God acting through human events which were important only insofar as they revealed the divine.

There might be more to say in praise of Johnson's book if he had been better read in allegory and more conscious of the artistic problems it presents. Those problems are often too much for him. He is unable to sustain his tone. Faced with a variety of stubborn facts to record, he often sets them down in literal terms, forgetting all about Christ's armies; again, he is so caught up by enthusiasm for his vision of New England's progress as God's triumph that he blurs or quite submerges the tale of events, some concrete presentation of which is necessary if his readers are to share anything of his excitement. His very enthusiasm drives him into formless sentences, obviously written with eagerness but losing their effect because the words are allowed to tumble out just as they came to mind. The shapelessness of much of his prose comes, no doubt, also from the fact that he was a layman and not a university man or a theological scholar. The best Puritan prose is characterized by its orderly structure, and its clarity comes from its reliance on logical rules. Johnson is a good example of how important the logic and order of Puritan style were, for although the best qualities of his prose are characteristic of Puritan writing, the worst seem to arise from his neglect or ignorance of principles upon which his more scholarly contemporaries insisted.

Near the beginning of his "Wonder-Working Providence," Johnson writes:

> In this very time Christ the glorious King of his Churches, raises an Army out of our English Nation, for freeing his people from their long servitude under usurping Prelacy; and because every corner of England was filled with the fury of malignant adversaries, Christ creates a New England to muster up the first of his Forces in; Whose low condition, little number, and remotenesse of place made these adversaries triumph, despising this day of small things, but in this hight of their pride the Lord Christ brought sudden, and unexpected destruction upon them. Thus have you a touch of the time when this worke began.[39]

Here the military allegory is plain; so, especially in the weak conclusion of his paragraph, are the tentativeness and looseness of Johnson's prose.

Another passage shows the use of the same conception of the Puritans as soldiers of Christ. It also illustrates the characteristic Puritan fondness for relating the adventures of New Englanders to those of the people of Israel, and the Puritan's constant reliance on the imagery of the Bible.

> Who would not be a Souldier on Christs side, where is such a certainty of victory? nay I can tell you a farther word of encouragement, every true-hearted Souldier that falls by the sword in this fight, shall not lye dead long, but stand upon his feet again, and be made partaker of the triumph of this Victory: and none can be overcome but by turning his back in fight. And for a word of terrour to the enemy, let them know, Christ will never give over the raising of fresh Forces, till they are overthrown root and branch. And now you antient people of Israel

look out of your Prison grates, let these Armies of the Lord Christ
Jesus provoke you to acknowledge he is certainly come, I and
speedily he doth come to put life into your dry bones: here is a
people not onely praying but fighting for you, that the great
block may be removed out of the way, (which hath hindered
hitherto) that they with you may enjoy that glorious resurrec-
tion-day, the glorious nuptials of the Lamb: when not only the
Bridegroom shall appear to his Churches both of Jews and Gentiles, (which are his spouse) in a more brighter array than ever
heretofore, but also his Bride shall be clothed by him in the
richest garments that ever the Sons of men put on, even the
glorious graces of Christ Jesus, in such a glorious splendor to the
eyes of man, that they shall see and glorifie the Father of both
Bridegroom and Bride.[40]

For all his stylistic faults and the breathless confusion of his worst paragraphs, Johnson's enthusiasm
shines through much of his prose and goes far to disarm
criticism of his technical defects. Here and there he
managed to give adequate expression, if no more, to his
pictorial sense of history and to the warm emotion with
which he wrote:

As the Lord surrounded his chosen Israel with dangers deepe
to make his miraculous deliverance famous throughout, and to
the end of the World, so here behold the Lord Christ, having
egged a small handfull of his people forth in a forlorne Wilder-
nesse, stripping them naked from all humane helps, plunging
them in a gulph of miseries, that they may swim for their lives
through the Ocean of his Mercies, and land themselves safe in
the armes of his compassion.[41]

Such sentences as this bear witness to the depth and dignity of Johnson's feeling for history as the handmaiden
of religious truth.

Further evidence as to the Puritans' belief in the importance of history appears everywhere in their writings. One of the necessary virtues of a minister was "prudence," and Puritan spokesmen linked together moral philosophy and history as teachers of it.[42] But the chief benefit of history was its demonstration of the omnipotence and immediacy of God's control of all affairs of earth, and of his special care for the righteous among men. The emphasis on "special providences" — conspicuous cases of what seemed to be God's direct intervention in human concerns — and on the whole providential interpretation of history, increases markedly as the seventeenth century advances.

The pioneer Puritans like Bradford had little need to labor the doctrine of providence. Their contemporaries accepted it and were ostensibly at least all adventurers devoted to God's service. But as the first generation in New England gave way to the second, there was less of pioneer fervor, less of the spiritual excitement that had animated the founding fathers. This, of course, terrified the ministers, who saw that they must find means to revive the pristine Puritan zeal. They believed that if their flocks could be reawakened to a sense that God held them in the hollow of his hand, a desire to sacrifice everything to the doing of God's will might be revived. They believed that if the story of the hardships and heroism of the pioneer settlers was properly told, only the hardest-hearted sinner could remain untouched, and every man with a spark of proper feeling would try to live in a fashion worthy of those who had gone before. History could therefore be a way of stirring up a generation grown sluggish in religion, and not long after the middle of the seventeenth century it became a matter of public policy to encourage historians to write. In the 1660's, the Plymouth colony granted £25 from public funds to pay for the printing of a history of the colony, and when the book appeared "a barrell of marchantable beefe" was added as a bonus.[43] In 1673 a Massachusetts minister declared:

> God hath shewn us almost unexampled unparall[el]ed mercy. And it were very well if there were a memorial of these things faithfully drawn up, and transmitted to Posterity . . . It is our great duty to be the Lords *Remembrancers* or *Recorders* . . . It is a desireable thing, that all the loving kindnesses of God, and his singular favours . . . might be Chronicled and communicated (in the History of them) to succeeding Ages.[44]

Later the colonial legislators voted that it was "necessary, & a duty incumbent upon us, to take due notice of all occurrances & passages of God's providence towards the people of this jurisdiction since their first arrivall in these parts," and £50 was granted to the Reverend William Hubbard for the manuscript of his history of New England, finished by 1682.[45] There could be no better indication of the extent to which the Puritan thought of history as an ally of religion.

The result of the Plymouth colony's interest in the publication of its story was Nathaniel Morton's *New Englands Memoriall*, printed at Cambridge in 1669. Morton was William Bradford's nephew and his book is little more than an epitome of his uncle's work, which was still in manuscript. *New Englands Memoriall* has no marked literary merit, but it does show plainly that by 1669 the Puritans were consciously using history, interpreted in terms of God's providence, as an incentive to righteousness, and were celebrating the heroes of the earliest days of the colony in order that their sons might be aroused to serve God worthily in their turn.

This is apparent if Morton's text is compared with Bradford's. For the most part the younger man slavishly follows the elder, but in one respect Morton goes beyond his source. Bradford winds up his account of 1622, "Hear with I end this year," but Morton says: "And herewith I end the Relation of the most Remarkable Passages of Gods Providence towards the first Planters, which fell out in this Year." Discussing the events of 1625 Morton is not content with his uncle's reflection that "Gods judgments are unsearchable," but prefaces the passage in question with, "And here I may not omit the observable dispensation of Gods providence." [46]

Elsewhere Morton hammers the same note. His dedication to Governor Thomas Prince begins: "The consideration of the weight of Duty that lieth upon us, to Commemorize to future Generations the memorable passages of Gods Providence to us and our Predecessors in the beginning of this Plantation, hath wrought in me a restlesness of spirit, and earnest desire, that something might be atchieved in that behalf, more (or at least otherwise) then as yet hath been done." [47] In his preface "To the Christian Reader" he repeats:

I have for some length of time looked upon it as a duty incumbent, especially on the immediate Successors of those that have
had so large Experience of those many memorable and signall
Demonstrations of Gods goodness, *viz.* The first Beginners of this
Plantation in *New England*, to commit to writing his gracious
dispensations on that behalf; having so many inducements there-
unto, not onely otherwise, but so plentifully in the Sacred Scriptures.[48]

And Morton's attempt to fit his chronicle into a larger
historical picture appears in the opening paragraph of
the *Memoriall,* where he says:

It is the usuall manner of the Dispensation of the Majesty of
Heaven, to work wonderfully by weak means for the effectuating
of great things, to the intent that he may have the more Glory
to himself: Many instances hereof might be produced, both out
of the Sacred Scriptures, and common Experience; and amongst
many others of this kinde, the late Happy and Memorable Enter-
prize of the Planting of that part of *America* called *New-England*, deserveth to be Commemorized to future Posterity.[49]

Certainly Morton took pains to emphasize the providential interpretation of history more than Bradford
had done. Also, of course, he praised the pioneer colonists as examples for all their God-fearing successors.
In a single sentence he sums up not only the motive of
his own book, but one of the basic purposes of historical
writing as the Puritans conceived of it. The ends which
he thought history served were, "That God may have
his due praise, His Servants the Instruments have their
Names embalmed, and the present and future Ages may
have the fruit and benefit of Gods great work."[50]

Still another phase of the Puritans' dedication of historical writing to the stimulation of piety is shown with special vividness in their histories of their encounters with the Indians, particularly the disastrous King Philip's War of 1675 and 1676. The colonists were, to be sure, victorious, but only after heavy losses, and, according to Puritan preachers, rather by God's providential mercy than by their own prowess. "As to *Victoryes* obtained," said Increase Mather, "we have no cause to glory in any thing that we have done, but rather to be ashamed and confounded for our own wayes . . . God hath let us see that he could easily have destroyed us" and "hath convinced us that we our selves could not subdue" the Indians.[51] From the ministerial point of view the war made it necessary to seek out the colonists' sins which had provoked God's wrath, and it was not hard to find a considerable list. Immodest dress, wearing of periwigs by men, drunkenness, profanity, sabbath breaking, labor disputes, all marked the backsliding of New England, which God had punished by war. Even those who were lukewarm in religion must have been shocked by the extent of the punishment; more than a dozen towns in Massachusetts alone were laid waste. Here was a chance for the pious historian, and several writers seized it. By telling the tragic story of the war as the tale of how God, in the Old Testament manner, chastened his chosen, they might frighten and impress some of the colonists who had forgotten, or had become indifferent to, their duty toward an Almighty, implacable, watchful, and just.

The war was hardly over before Increase Mather

brought out a history of it, obviously designed to recall New England's sinners from their evil ways. But the fact that a Puritan wrote history to drive home a moral did not mean that he gave up his standards of accuracy. Mather says: "I hope that in one thing (though it may be in little else) I have performed the part of an *Historian,* viz. In endeavouring to relate things truly and impartially." Of some books of the Bible he asks, "What were these Books but the faithful" — the word is important — "*Records* of the Providential Dispensations of God in the Days of old? . . . It is proper for the Ministers of God, to engage themselves in services of this nature." [52]

Accordingly Mather's story of King Philip's War is everywhere directed toward providential interpretation, and he confesses that what he had chiefly in mind in writing it was the "Exhortation," which is really a separate section at the end. This is a direct attack on the shortcomings of New England. Mather was sure that unless there were prompt reforms, God would heap more calamities on the colonists. He was both historian and preacher; and his book illustrates admirably the way in which, particularly in the latter part of the seventeenth century, history was used in New England to castigate the present as well as to praise the past.

The Puritan's fundamental attitude toward literature is nowhere more sharply revealed than in his historical endeavors. All literature was for him a means to a useful end, and the most useful of all ends was, of course, to teach religious truth and to incite readers to

follow God. Hundreds and hundreds of Puritan sermons show in every paragraph the Puritan's eagerness
to put literature to work in the cause of righteousness;
so do a variety of pious tracts and expositions of doctrine; so do his histories. They are stamped on each
page with the marks of his pious zeal to edify, but this
does not mean that in writing them he forgot all about
art and allowed no place for imagination or emotion.
Once the Puritan was sure that a pious purpose could
be served by writing, he set all his literary skill to work.
In his historical writing the results were often surprisingly good, even by the standards of our time. The
Puritan's belief that history was the tangible record of
God's power called upon him for all the seriousness and
dignity and strength of his best prose. His imaginative
identification of himself with a great myth, extending
from the events of Genesis to the most recent Indian fight
on the Massachusetts frontier, gave vividness and excitement to his tale of the adventures of the New England pioneers. There are in colonial histories many examples of the Puritan's powers as an artist, and many
pages which recreate in moving terms the robust atmosphere of a truly heroic New England. It was a New
England in which strong men fought and suffered and
died courageously, because they were committed, emotionally and intellectually, to a life of faith.

IV

THE "PERSONAL LITERATURE"
OF THE PURITANS

BEHIND the Puritan's conception of history, and at the very root of his thinking, was his conviction that all religious progress centered on the individual. The foundation of religious life was his search for faith, his struggle to do the divine will in order to fulfill his part of a covenant, and to achieve some assurance that God would spare him in the end. He was a pilgrim from adversity to success, from sin toward blessedness. The history he liked best was the story of Puritanism as the advance of a group and the search of a society for salvation, but he recognized that the society and its success depended always on its devoted members.

It has been said that Puritanism is characterized by "the desire of the individual to stand alone and accept responsibility, and a belittling of all material and adventitious props in exercising this responsibility." [1] The emphasis put by the Puritan preacher on the individual's walk with God has been often noticed. Wherever possible, theological abstractions were related to the concrete facts of personal experience, and doctrine was explained in terms of the individual life. Predestination, election, and sanctification were taught with constant reference to their bearing on human lives, which were conceived of as pilgrimages from the limbo of the unawakened to the glory vouchsafed to the regenerate. There was no better way to exemplify spiritual progress concretely than to write the biographies of the righteous. Accordingly, the Puritans were always interested in personal experience and eager to have full records of it. They measured their own lives and those of their friends and leaders by a spiritual pattern, and to make measurement possible, kept diaries, wrote autobiographies, and recorded all that they could learn about the lives of those who seemed to them worthy of imitation and praise.

At the base of the pyramid of the Puritan "personal literature" in New England are the diaries, the informal records of the pious settlers' daily life. In spite of the ravages of centuries of New England house cleaning, movings, and fires, hundreds of them survive, in manuscript or in print. It is striking that the colonists, engrossed in politics, toiling in the woods or fields, drilling with the train-bands, going to church, building schools and a college, opening roads and founding towns, keeping shops, and maintaining homes and raising families under what now seem unbearably difficult conditions, so often took precious minutes at the end of their arduous days to set down an account of them. Of course, the habit of diary-keeping has always been very common, but the Puritan in the colonies and in England was especially given to it. So far as we can judge, Puritan communities in the seventeenth century produced more diaries than did other groups, and the reasons for this go back directly to the Puritan's way of belief.

He was naturally concerned with keeping an account of his acts and thoughts in order that it might serve as a clue to his progress in his absorbing personal quest for some assurance of salvation. Events as such were not his chief interest; what was closest to his heart was the service a diary might be in showing him his own faults and virtues, in keeping fresh in his memory what he learned each day about himself and about his relation to God's law, and in helping him to devote all his energies to divinely approved ends. But he was interested, too, in keeping track of what happened in his little world, because the smallest incident might be an indication of God's attitude toward his servants and their ways.

The Puritan, especially the Puritan in New England, conceived of the process of regeneration as ordinarily a slow one, and one that involved patience and effort on the part of the individual. There must be study, a search for advice from the learned and godly, constant striving for righteous conduct, and persistent self-scrutiny. Obviously, since the process was one of immense importance it was worth examining, and the central motive of many Puritan diarists seems to have been to insure that every relevant detail of their progress toward God should be available for their own instruction and guidance, just as a set of orderly accounts instructs and guides a merchant as to the success or failure of his affairs. John Beadle, an English Puritan preacher, made the point clear when he pointed out that governments have to keep daily records of their actions, tradesmen keep "shop books, merchants their accounts, lawyers their books of precedents and physicians theirs of experiments, wary heads of households their records of daily disbursements and travelers theirs of things seen and endured." [2] A good Christian had an even greater need for daily notes, since his chief business was with God.

There was a further motive for the Puritan diarist. It is recognized that some form of confessional practice is commonly associated with intense religious feeling. Whether we choose to phrase the fact in psychological or in theological terms, it seems plain that many men and women need some way of escape from the strain of inner conflicts and emotional disturbances, and find it often by externalizing at least momentarily the problems by which they are beset. The keeping of a diary is such an escape, or may be, for those who keep diaries with the earnestness of the Puritan. Samuel Pepys, the greatest of English diarists, was no Puritan and certainly no pathological introvert, but he found a necessary refuge from the stresses of his life in his detailed and amazingly frank record of it. A middle-class Englishman with middle-class prejudices, he saw enough of the gaieties of the Restoration court to be both shocked and tempted by them. He had decent standards and rudimentary moral aspirations, but he was often betrayed by his weak flesh. He had to discover how to live in a time of social and political turmoil without giving up either worldly rewards or patriotic principles. It was a satisfaction to him to display completely, even in shorthand and for no eyes but his own, the whole web of conflict in which he was involved. The satisfaction was so great that when his eyes failed and he could no longer keep his diary he wrote sadly that he must henceforth have it "kept by my people in long-hand, and must therefore be contented to set down no more than is fit for them and all the world to know . . . And so I betake myself to that course, which is almost as much as to see myself go into my grave." [3]

This was not hyperbole. For Pepys, as for many others before and since, some means of uninhibited confession is indispensable. The good Catholic still confesses to his priest. The Protestant may still talk freely to his minister about his problems and his hopes and fears and may go to him as much for a chance to talk as for advice. Even those who admit to no religious feeling rely on physicians and psychiatrists in a way essentially like that of the devout man at the confessional. And the seventeenth-century Puritan so needed some outlet for his doubts and fears that his diary was precious to him, and to be deprived of the chance to write in it would often have seemed to him, as it did to Pepys, a kind of half-death.

The nature of the Puritans' problem is implied in a few sentences of Helen White's:

The first half of the seventeenth century witnessed a pretty steady development of psychological self-awareness, of a disposition to inquire more closely than ever before into the life within.

At the same time, that lively sense of the potency of outside forces for the motivation and direction of the inner life, that had been so strong in the Middle Ages continued almost unabated. The result was that sense of the almost catastrophic hazard of the moral life that occasionally leaps from the tacit anxiety of the godly into direct expression.[4]

The Puritan, quite aware of advancing psychological knowledge and theologically disposed to self-scrutiny, certainly knew also about the potency of outside forces to affect the life within. England experienced, in the days of the Puritan colonization of Massachusetts, economic and social changes and dislocations from which the colonist could not wholly detach himself; it suffered even civil war. The colonist had the terrors of a great ocean to face and the dangers and hardships of a new settlement in a wilderness to surmount. He had to resist all sorts of temptations, all sorts of fears; he had to build a church and state in the face of opposition and to pattern a way of life that would work materially and yet involve no spiritual lapse for individual or group. The result was tension; out of the tension came many of the more robust qualities of the Puritan and also the desire for relief expressed in his confessional relation to his diary. In its pages he could reveal what otherwise he must have hidden, he could expose his heart to God, and in so doing he could get the satisfaction of expressing on the conscious level the fears and doubts which molested him and which, totally suppressed, could lead to dangerous and painful consequences.

This is what Michael Wigglesworth, colonial poet

and colonial divine, tried to do in his diary.[5] It is perhaps less a diary than a collection of observations on its author's spiritual ailments, since it is less a record of concrete events than an account of Wigglesworth's constant and tortured self-searchings. It is a highly personal document, obviously written only for his own eyes, and its most intimate revelations are set down in shorthand. Throughout, the emphasis is on Wigglesworth's failures as a Christian. His temptations, fears, doubts, and sins are meticulously described. He was frail physically and, probably as a result, abnormally introspective and apprehensive, and his remorseless self-analysis displays everywhere a pathological sensitiveness to his own shortcomings, coupled with an all too lively dread of how God might punish him for them. If he works hard with his books or his students and enjoys it, or preaches with what seems to him success, he worries lest he forget God in the carnal pleasure he finds in his labors. The slightest peccadillo is magnified to a major sin; the slightest adversity is reckoned as evidence of God's wrath. The result is a book that is painful to read because it seems unbearably morbid, the fruit of an obsessive sense of guilt. It is not wholly typical of the diaries written by most of his compatriots, but its traits are simply exaggerations of theirs, and like them, it has many poignant passages in which the sinner, overcome by a consciousness of sin, turns helplessly to God with an appeal for his mercy. Such an appeal, the Puritan was sure, was not likely to be heard unless it came from a man who recognized his own sinfulness and was struggling to purge himself of it. The process of confession in the pages of a diary was an aid to purgation as well as a relief, at least for the moment, from a gnawing inner sense of fear and despair. If the results seem to most readers repellent or incomprehensible, it is worth remembering that such pages as Wigglesworth's came from a passionate desire for holiness and were written only for the author and for God. It is worth remembering, too, that when Wigglesworth or any other Puritan "fell weary of the coil of business, discouraged by external difficulty, by the sense of his own failure, and by the futility of his own effort, he . . . poured his heart out in his diary. At such moment, the healthiest mind seems morbid." "The seeming morbidity" is "merely that of a hard-working idealist momentarily overwrought." [6] The New England Puritan was certainly "a hard-working idealist," and the more intense his faith and the more profound his yearning for salvation, the more frequent were the moments when he was overwrought.

Wigglesworth's diary has not been printed. Of the New England colonial diaries which have, the only two which have been at all widely read and the only two which have much claim on students of literature are those of Samuel Sewall and Cotton Mather.

Sewall's was kept in considerable detail over many years by one of the most active magistrates and businessmen in the colonies. It is sprinkled with delightful passages in which Sewall's shrewd observation of the men and events about him are couched in prose which, although always simple, is lively and direct in its phrasing. But Sewall, although pious, was rarely deeply introspective, and in his diary he was concerned rather with events and with the moral reflections they suggested than with the personal religious emotions characteristic of more devout Puritans. None the less, his pages were clearly dictated in part by his sense of the importance of keeping an account of God's management of the world and his conviction that even the most trivial occurrence might be a symbol of divine power. His effort seems to have been to find sanction for the practical concerns of his busy life by relating them to God's divine plan. He was handicapped by an essential worldliness that set him apart from the ministers and scholars who expressed most fully the basic religious attitudes of the colonists.

The authentic Puritan note sounds, however, in one of the most striking entries in his diary: "Morning proper fair, the wether exceedingly benign, but (to me) metaphoric, dismal, dark and portentous, some prodigie appearing in every corner of the skies." [7] Fair as the morning was, Sewall thought he felt within himself some divine stirring which made the autumn skies seem dismal, full of prodigies, serving as metaphors for God's power and the wrath to come. The Puritan strain is patent also in another passage sixteen months later. On March 19, 1677, Sewall writes:

Mr. Thacher [a minister] . . . told me I had liberty to tell what God had done for my soul. After I had spoken, prayed again. Before I came away told him my Temptations to him

alone, and bad him acquaint me if he knew anything by me that
might hinder justly my coming into Church. He said he thought
I ought to be encouraged, and that my stirring up to it was of
God.[8]

But two years afterward Sewall was still doubtful. "I
have been of a long time loth to enter into strict Bonds
with God," he writes, and then continues in a passage of
typical Puritan self-analysis:

Remember, since I had thoughts of joining to the Church, I
have been exceedingly tormented in my mind . . . sometimes
with my own unfitness and want of Grace: yet through impor-
tunity of friends, and hope that God might communicate himself to me in the ordinance, and because of my child (then hoped
for) its being baptised, I offered myself, and was not refused.[9]

When he was admitted to the church he read a formal
account of his faith, and wrote in his diary:

I resolved to confess what a great Sinner I had been, but going
on in the method of the Paper, it came not to my mind. And
now that Scruple of the Church vanished, and I began to be
more afraid of myself . . . And I could hardly sit down to the
Lord's Table. But I feared that if I went away I might be less
fit next time, and thought it would be strange for me who was
just then joined to the Church, to withdraw, wherefore I
stayed. But I never experienced more unbelief. I feared at least
that I did not believe there was such an one as Jesus Xt., and yet
was afraid that because I came to the ordinance without belief,
that for the abuse of Xt. I should be stricken dead; yet I had
some earnest desires that Xt. would, before the ordinance were
done, though it were where he was just going away, give me
some glimpse of himself; but I perceived none. Yet I seemed
then to desire the coming of the next Sacrament day, that I
might do better, and was stirred up hereby dreadfully to seek

God who many times before had touched my heart by Mr. Thacher's praying and preaching more than now. The Lord pardon my former grieving of his Spirit, and circumcise my heart to love him with all my heart and soul.[10]

Here is both the confessional and the spiritual book-keeping of a tormented soul in account with God.

The other of the two famous New England Puritan diaries, Cotton Mather's, is the work of a fanatically zealous Puritan minister. It is impossible to tell certainly whether it was kept by him for his own eyes alone, or whether he wrote it intending that it should some day become a public memorial to his piety, in which case, of course, it does not belong with typical Puritan diaries but represents a more deliberate and formal kind of work. Some passages certainly give the impression that Mather wrote it in order to exhibit himself in the best possible light, and his wailing over his sins seems too often to display a mind centered in self rather than in God.

But however it is judged, the diary does give an excellent further example of what the Puritan diarist was apt to write and why, and its theatrical heightening of the qualities found in other diaries makes clearer what those qualities were. Mather, sitting in his study, "found a strange Impression on" his mind, "intimating to me," he says,

that Heaven was willing to converse with me, after a very familiar Manner, if I would now look and wait in a suitable Posture for it. It was . . . said unto me, *Go into your great Chamber and I will speak with you!*

109

So I retired into a great Chamber of my House . . . and cast myself prostrate on the Floor before the Lord.

There I cried unto the Lord, with humble and bitter Confessions of my own Loathsomeness before Him, and abhorred myself as worthy to be thunderstruck into *Dust and Ashes*. For a while, I had no other Expansions of Soul, than in all Devotions. But at length, I felt an inexpressible *Afflatus* come from Heaven upon my mind, which dissolved me into a Flood of Tears, that ran down upon the Floor . . . This Conversation with Heaven, left a sweet, a calm, a considerate, a sanctifying, an Heavenly Impression upon my Soul."

Few Puritans, probably, had such direct "conversations with Heaven," and fewer would have admitted it if they had, lest they be accused of Antinomian pretensions to direct revelation. At the same time, Cotton Mather's record, however blown up by his own fancy, must have had its origin in a kind of feeling that many Puritans often had in some form, even though they rarely attempted to describe it in their diaries.

If Cotton Mather was not actually writing an informal personal record but a work that he planned for the eyes of other readers, it forms a natural link between the diary as such, and the more elaborate and conscious journals and autobiographies written by many Puritans. The diary was for its author's own use, but if he took time to select from it, to revise its hastily written paragraphs, and to cast the result into coherent form, he might make the material useful not only to himself but to others. The result would be an autobiography, and its virtue would be that it might teach other men, also engaged in the fight for godliness, something of the way in which that fight was apt to go. If every good man was a pilgrim toward blessedness, the best guidebooks might be accounts of how others had fared on the road toward Heaven. Bunyan's *Grace Abounding* has achieved its place as an English religious classic because of the imagination and stylistic skill with which its author dramatizes his own spiritual struggle, so that the book can be read with excitement even by those who profess no religious faith, provided they have any experience of inner conflict or any realization of how the pursuit of an exalted aim may tax the best energies of heart and mind. No other Puritan achieved what Bunyan did in autobiography because no other Puritan had his special talent for the task, but many attempted to do the same thing.

One example from New England will suffice. Thomas Shepard, a Cambridge graduate, came to this country in 1635 and became minister at Newtown, now Cambridge. Some time after settling there he composed an autobiography, covering his life up to 1637. It was based on a diary, but as it stands it is clearly a careful composition designed to be read by those whom it might help. That appears plainly in Shepard's dedication of it to his son: "To my deare son . . . with whom I leave these records of gods great kindnes to him not knowing that I shall live to tell them my selfe with my own mouth, that so he may learne to know & love the great & most high god: the god of his father." [12]

The first nine pages tell how God saved the Shepards from shipwreck twice, when they first tried to sail to Massachusetts; how Thomas, the younger, was safely born in spite of an accident to his mother; how he was gravely sick, and how his father prayed for him with a systematic list of arguments to convince God that the child should be preserved. The plea was heard, and the Shepards started their voyage again. Sickness, accidents, and storm were safely endured, and then, in Massachusetts, young Thomas was threatened by blindness. Once more God saved him "suddenly & strangely," almost "miraculously." This section of the manuscript ends with the elder Shepard's apostrophe: "Now consider my son of this care of god for thee & remember to lift up thy eyes to heaven to god in everlasting prayses of him & dependance upon him, & take heed thou dost not make thy eyes windowes of lust; but give thy eyes nay thy hart & whole soule & body to him that hath bin so carefull of thee when thou couldst not care for thy selfe." [13] God's providence had protected a child; surely that child should dedicate himself to God.

The autobiography proper begins with Shepard's account of his troubled boyhood. The plague visited the English village in which he was born, and he was sent off to live with his grandparents. His mother died and his father was married again "to another woman who . . . let" Shepard "see the difference betweene" his "own mother & a stepmother." "Shee did seeme not to love me," Shepard says, and adds, "it may be that it was justly also for my childishnes." For a good Puritan, unhappiness, even as affecting a child, was wherever possible to be read as a "just" corrective. A harsh schoolmaster discouraged Shepard from learning and he often wished he could "keepe hogs or beasts rather than goe to Schoole." His father fell sick, and the boy prayed "very strongly & hartily . . . & made some covenant if god would" save the elder Shepard, the younger would "serve him the better." But God did not listen, and at ten young Shepard was an orphan, committed to his stepmother's care. She neglected his education, but his brother intervened, and a minister waked Thomas up to "a love & desire of the honour of learning." God helped directly too, when Shepard could not take good notes on sermons he heard. He prayed, and "the next sabboth was able to take notes." Then came Cambridge University and a period of neglect of God and of foolish pride in displaying scholarship. But just when Shepard "was most vile," and immediately after he had narrowly escaped death from smallpox, "the Lord began to Call" him "home to the fellowship of his grace." [14]

Such calling is always a strategic point in Puritan autobiography, and Shepard devotes as much space to describing his experience at this time as he does to his whole earlier life. He dilates on his sins, especially on his drinking, and tells of a Sunday morning when, in his own words, "I awakened late . . . sick with my beastly carriage . . . I . . . went out into the feelds & there spent that sabboth lying hid in the corne . . . where the Lord who might justly have cut me off in the mids of my sin; did meet me with much sadnes of hart & troubled my soule for this & other my sins which then I had cause & leysure to thinke of." The Calvinist God was a stern judge; but it should be remembered that to the Puritan He could seem tender — and there is a touching expression of this in Shepard's "Now when I was woorst he began to be best unto me." [15]

Shepard emphasizes the importance of meditation and, especially, self-analysis and the recording of experience:

My cheefe meditation was about the evill of sin, the terrour of gods wrath, day of death, bewty of Christ, the deceiptfulnes of the hart; &c. but principally I found this my misery, sin was not my greatest evill, did ly light upon me as yet, yet I was much afrayd of death & the flames of gods wrath; & this I remember I never went out to meditate in the feelds, but I did find the Lord teaching me somewhat of my selfe or himselfe or the vanity of the woorld, I never saw before; & hence I tooke out a little booke I have every day into the feelds & writ down what god taught me least I should forget them. [16]

Out of his fears and temptations and in spite of his inability to feel sin as the greatest evil, Shepard came safely at last to confident faith. But in the ministry to which he turned naturally, he fell foul of the Anglican bishops, and became virtually a fugitive in exile from the church. New England seemed a refuge, and he meticulously listed the reasons which "swayed" him to emigrate. The exodus from England, like the Biblical Exodus — Shepard spoke of "the god that brought me out of Egipt" — was to be signalized by "the Lord's woonderfull terrour & mercy." [17] For many pages the autobiography is devoted to the hardships, narrow escapes, and providential mercies visited upon the Shepard family in their journey to Massachusetts Bay.

Once in New England, Shepard found more troubles — Indian wars and the disturbance caused in Massachusetts churches by Anne Hutchinson and her Antinomian "enthusiasts." But he recognized trials as part of God's plan for him. He thanked the Lord for carrying him to "a land of peace tho a place of tryall," and remarked, certainly without resentment or repining, "The Lord hath not bin woont to let me live long without some affliction or other." The autobiography ends with the touching story of the death of Shepard's wife, leading to the final and key sentence of the whole, "Thus God hath visited & scourged me for my sins & sought to weane me from this woorld, but I have ever found it a difficult thing to profit ever but a little by the sorest & sharpest afflictions." [18]

This statement unifies the entire autobiography. It is, of course, a personal record of one man's life, but it is shaped to a larger theme — God's dealing with errant man. For Puritan readers its value was twofold: it was the record of a good man's life, rich in suggestion as to how a human heart might triumph over doubt, fear, and sin, if properly receptive to God's grace; and it was in effect a sermon on adversity as a stimulus to holiness. For Puritan readers it was exciting because it was a record of the world they knew, and of a man they revered; it was, as the typical Puritan autobiography and indeed most Puritan literature always was, an interpretation of the divine in terms easily grasped by men.

Shepard's style was informal, but vivid by virtue of its simple phrasing and diction; neither elaborately rhetorical nor figurative, but lighted up by pictorial details and by a few metaphors and figures which are none the less effective because they are drawn either from the Bible or from the commonest stuff of everyday life. A town in which Shepard lived for part of his boyhood was "a most blind town & corner," and there he was "put to keepe geese & other such cuntry woorke." Shepard gives thanks that the Lord "plucked" him "out of that sinke & Sodom," "the prophane ignorant . . . Towcester" where he was born.[19] His soul suffers from "3 mayne wounds"; in his unregenerate state, he says, "I could do nothing but I did seeke myselfe in it & was imprisoned there." "The terrours of god began to breake in lik floods of fire" into his soul. "I did see god," Shepard writes, "like a Consuming fire & an everlasting burning & my selfe like a poor prisoner leading to that fire." [20] In style as in matter his story was attuned to its audience.

The Puritan autobiography, as Shepard's shows, was a more formal work than the diary, sufficiently shaped and interpreted so that through it there might be communicated to others whatever was useful and edifying in its subject. The third type of Puritan "personal literature" — biography — represents a further formalization.

For the Puritan, biographies or autobiographies of good men were "Flags of Mercy before a Company of Rebels to win them in." [21] The figure expresses admirably the central motive for Puritan "personal literature." Puritans knew quite well what rebels in arms were and how on occasion a flag of truce might win over some of them from rebellion. Could not a rebel against God, an unregenerate man, walking in darkness and closing his heart and mind to divine truth, be brought back to join the faithful if at the right time a "Flag of Mercy" were displayed so that he could not fail to see it? And what better "Flag of Mercy" than a story of how this or that good man had come by God's grace out of terror and doubts into peace and assurance through faith? An autobiography or a biography might give a sinner precisely the impulse he needed to make him seek God and, by striving to join the faithful, possibly to win his share of God's amazing gifts. "A Flag of Mercy" was a practical implement of war, not a decorative banner; it was a sign that must above all be visible and understandable, and details of its embroidery mattered not at all compared to boldness and clarity of design. It was more essential to Puritan biography that its meaning be grasped than that it display its writer's skill. This means, of course, that Puritan biographies were at bottom didactic, works of piety, and that they aimed less at the modern ideal of accurate revelation of a personality than at the graphic portrayal of the virtues of the Puritan saint. But unless the story of a life were told dramatically and vividly enough to hold the reader's attention, and unless its structure and style were such as to make its useful message clear, it was no real "Flag of Mercy." A rebel could be drawn into camp only by a sign which he could not ignore.

The biographies written in seventeenth-century New

England are, then, all primarily works of religious edification. Most of them were clearly designed for publication. The autobiography was usually circulated in manuscript among a family and a group of friends, since there were obvious dangers that a man who made public the story of his own life might seem to be sinfully exalting himself. But a biography of one good Puritan by another served an essential purpose and ran no risk of seeming to be the product of personal vanity. It was, moreover, a form of writing recognized as valuable even by those who were not primarily pious. Bacon, in his *Advancement of Learning,* had called for more "lives" of important men, and such seventeenth-century writers as Izaak Walton, Thomas Fuller, and, later, Gilbert Burnet and Richard Baxter testify to their century's interest in biography. Naturally the New Englander tried his hand at writing in a form so plainly sanctioned by current tastes and, for his purposes, so useful in spreading piety.

There were material obstacles, of course, in the way of any large harvest of biography from Puritan New England. Type and paper were expensive and printers few. What was published was what seemed most useful, and however valuable biography was, sermons, theological expositions, and contributions to the defense of New England Puritanism against its enemies came first. Some New England books were printed in England, but obviously an account by a New Englander of a New England worthy was not often likely to sell widely in London. Thus few New England biographies were printed until at the end of the seventeenth century Cotton Mather sent off to the press his great tome, the *Magnalia Christi Americana,* which contains a large collection of "lives," long and short, used as foundation stones for Mather's interpretation of colonial religious history.

Like most Puritan biographies, Mather's were fundamentally case-histories. Since regeneration was usually not a lightning-stroke from on high but something achieved only after testing by confusion and fear, the process of "conversion" took many forms. There were manifold "varieties of religious experience," and to understand the basis for them, it was necessary to learn all the outward symptoms. From the Puritan standpoint, biography should be shaped by a theological principle in which divine election, vocation, justification, and, finally, salvation were crucial aspects of the dynamic operation of God's plan. If that plan was to be symbolized concretely in the tale of a man's life, the climactic episodes must be synchronized with those aspects.

The allegiance to theological concepts did not, however, require sterile formality, cold rule, or a lifeless pattern. Whatever else the Puritan biographer may have been, he was almost always emotionally concerned with his task and wrote not merely because it was a correct or useful thing to do, but because he genuinely and passionately admired his subject and the Puritan virtues which it exemplified. The eulogistic tone, inevitable in works written primarily to set up models of holiness, easily becomes tiresome, but Puritan biographies are not unexciting to those who can sympathize with the spiritual adventures of others and recognize the fundamental drama in the age-old struggle of aspiring man imprisoned by his own frailty and by the intractability of the material world. They derive vitality from the Puritan's deep conviction that in the individual life was the most tangible symbol of divine values. Generations of preachers, even before the seventeenth century, had taught plain men to understand theology in terms of the individual's quest for blessedness; the myth which turned life into a pilgrimage was deeply rooted in Puritan hearts. In biography the myth and the reality, the symbol and the fact, correspond. It is small wonder that Puritan biographies often communicate more directly than his other writings an actual sense of the faith by which the Puritan lived, of the things he saw as good, and of the hardships, fears, and dangers against which he fought his way toward truth.

The first New England religious biography to be printed was John Norton's *Abel being Dead yet speaketh*, a life of John Cotton, published in London in 1658. John Norton was a scholar and an austere one; John Cotton was one of the great saints of early New England. The modern reader longs for more vivid and homely picturing of Cotton as a personality, apart from his virtues and his labors in his pulpit and study, but even so, Norton's little book illustrates admirably some of the best qualities of Puritan "lives."

One of its purposes, of course, was to commemorate the good deeds of a pious man, not simply as a proper tribute to past greatness, but as an immediate means of stirring up his successors to seek holiness in their turn. "It is the priviledg of the blessed who lived in Heaven, whilst they livd on Earth; That they may live on Earth, whilst they live in Heaven." Norton wanted Cotton to "live on Earth" in the pages of a book, even after he had gone to Heaven, because it was "blessed" to remember the "Just." [22] Characteristically, the Bible is brought in for support:

A considerable part of the Scripture is a divine testimony of what the Faithful have done and suffered, recorded unto succeeding Generations, not only as a memorial of them, but as so many practical demonstrations of the Faithfulness of God: as so many full and glorious triumphs over the World, Sin and Satan, obtained by persons in like temptations, and subject to like passions with our selves. [23]

And on the central importance of the individual life, Norton says:

The greatest Object out of Heaven is the life and death of such upon Earth, who are now in Heaven . . . What God hath done for the Soul of the least Saint . . . would make a volume full of temptations, signes, and wonders: A wonderful History, because a History of such experiences, each one whereof is more then a Wonder. No greater acts then their obedience, both Active and Passive unto the death. [24]

From time to time the story is halted to list parallels between Cotton's doings and those of Biblical heroes. The method is cumbrous but the intent is clear, and no doubt the effect on Norton's readers was good. Cotton at one stage of his life was "exercised with some inward troubles which much dejected him"; then come the parallels:

No sooner had Christ received his mission into his publick ministery, but he is led into the wilderness to be tempted of the Devil. Wise *Heman* suffered the horrors of God, and was laid in the lowest pit. The Doctor of the Gentiles stood in need of being buffeted by Satan. The Tempter is in Christs hand, and an instrumental winnower of the Disciples.[25]

More significant still is this: "[God] transplants many of his Faithfull servants into this vast Wilderness . . . God giveth *Moses* the pattern of the Tabernacle in the Wilderness. *Ezekiel* seeth the formes of the House in exile. *John* receiveth his Revelation in *Patmos*." [26] On other pages, Norton cites other cases of God's care for his children in the wilderness, and it is easy to see why. The New England colonists were in a sense exiles, their country was still largely a wilderness, but were they not God's chosen, and would not God protect them as he had protected the faithful of yore?

Hence comes a special feature of New England biographies — the attention they give to the migration from Old England to New. Often the individual's motives for emigration are discussed about as seriously as the details of his conversion — and reasonably, since to come to Massachusetts was for a Puritan not only a decisive step in practical terms, but in his spiritual life a response to a special divine call. The stories of the voyages also are retailed at length, because just as Egypt might be a metaphor for England and New England might be a new Canaan, the Atlantic Ocean might be, for symbolic purposes, the Red Sea.

The emphasis in Norton's biography, as in all typical Puritan biographies, is on moral traits. What is said of Cotton's doings is used to illustrate his learning, diligence, meekness, hospitality, and the other qualities which made him famous and beloved. His death is carefully described because the way in which a man died might often prove, to fellow-Puritans at least, that he had been elected to salvation. For the modern reader the Cotton of the biography is painfully perfect, but in spite of that he preserves more individuality than do most of the heroes of earlier pious "lives" in England.

Those "lives" had been for the most part mere flat representations of a man's deeds, selected and presented to illustrate his typical quality as an exponent of this or that virtue. Such writing was useful, no doubt, but it reduced individuals to types, and it rarely achieved anything like rounded biographical portraiture. There was little to distinguish between one exemplar of chastity, self-sacrifice, or whatever virtue was being preached, and anyone else who behaved in the same way; one saint appeared much like another on the printed page. The old stereotyped patterns continued in many "lives" long after Norton's day, but there were also English seventeenth-century writers — from some of whom he may have learned — whose work shows a distinct advance in biographical technique.

That advance came primarily because, for a variety of reasons, biography, in something like the modern sense, seemed to the seventeenth century a useful art. Scientists and philosophers, excited by new discoveries and eager to learn more about the whole physical world, inevitably tried to understand the nature of men's minds, both because these were parts of physical reality and because it was obviously idle to try to systematize and methodize knowledge without some comprehension of what knowledge was and how the mind could arrive at it. Biography was a possible source of help if it could display not only actions but something of the mental life of the individual — if, in modern phraseology, it concerned itself with the psychological aspects of its subjects. The religious interests of the century, especially those of the Puritans, worked often in the same direction and tended more and more to emphasize the importance of biography. Protestantism put new emphasis on the individual, and the Puritan, as the most extreme Protestant, constantly thought of true godliness as the individual's struggle to transform himself completely into a servant of God. That he could achieve only through faith. Faith was, therefore, the final test of holiness, and although a man's deeds might give some evidence a man's essential sainthood must be measured by his motives, impulses, thoughts, and emotions as well as by his acts. The Puritan's interest in his own spiritual welfare and that of others made him so curious about all phases of spiritual experience that biography, if it was to satisfy him, could not be limited to external events or mere records of behavior.

The seventeenth century's increasing interest in widening and deepening the scope of biography demanded experimentation with new techniques. Anecdotes were used as sidelights on character. Direct discourse was common so that the subject might speak, or seem to speak, for himself. Excerpts from letters and diaries appeared in order that the reader might come as close as possible to the living quality of the subject. Both in Old England and in New, the writer of "lives" found new instruments ready to his hand, and some of them Norton used in his account of Cotton. Although that book is so frankly a work of edification and so patently the work of a scholar rather than an artist that it makes less use of such devices than many contemporary and later Puritan biographies, there are in it hints of relatively modern biographical method.

For an example of an anecdote used to illustrate character: "One of his Hearers . . . following him home after his publick labors in the Assembly . . . telling him that his Ministry was become either dark, or flat: He gently answered, *Both, Brother!* without further opening his mouth in his defence." [27] And the story of Cotton's deathbed is touching because of its realism: "Perceiving his departure to be at hand, and having nothing to do, only that great work of dying in the Lord, he totally composed and set himself for his dissolution, desiring that he might be permitted to improve the little remnant of his life without any . . .

impediment to his private devotions, and divine soliloquies between God and his Soul." [28] This is general and perhaps flat, but what follows suddenly brings the scene to life because it is centered on specific and evocative detail: "For that end he caused the Curtains to be drawn: and a Gentleman and brother of the Congregation that was much with him, and ministred unto him in his sickness, to promise him, that the Chamber should be kept private. But a while after, hearing the whispering of some brethren in the room, he called for that Gentleman, saying, Why do you break your word with me?" [29]

Norton's style is, on the whole, that of an erudite and rhetorically precise scholar, but there are, none the less, flashes of typical Puritan homeliness of diction and imagery. "His youth was unstained, whence he was so much the more capable of being an excellent Instrument in the Church in his after-age . . . The gratefulnese of the most excellent liquor unto the stomach, depends in part upon the quality of the vessel." [30] "The Hen which brings not forth without uncessant sitting night and day, is an apt Embleme of Students." [31] "It was Religion to him, both to run, and to run lawfully within the white lines and boundaries of his . . . race." [32] "So able an Opponent" in controversy "was rare; so candid an Opponent more rare. He that fell into his hands, was likely to fall soft enough." [33] "The non-resistance and softness of the Wooll breaks the force of the Cannon, and so saveth both the bullet and it self." [34] "The sword that is good metal will bow to the hilts, and yet come strait again. No metal more solid then gold, no metal more yielding under the hammer." [35] Norton — and most Puritans — accented narrative by colloquial phrasing and by "apt Emblemes," fitting metaphors and similes, to make their meaning crystal clear. Liquor and the pewter and clay from which it was drunk, field sports, hens, wrestlers, the wadding of the charge in a cannon, gold-beating, and the flexibility of a fine sword — these were things out of the everyday experience of Norton's readers, and his use of them to explain and illustrate moral qualities and divine truth was, for his audience, skillful and effective.

A dozen years after Norton's life of Cotton was printed there came out in Boston another biography, the life of Richard Mather by his son Increase. It is eulogistic of course, but it is a pleasant little book, lighted up by bits of direct discourse, by an anecdote or two, and by a few passages in which there is clearly an effort toward character analysis. Sprinkled throughout are excerpts from Richard Mather's private papers and from his journal, and those parts of his will which display his humility before God and his love for his children are used for a conclusion. In the only modern edition the book fills fifty-three pages. Four cover the story of Mather's life before his conversion, nine tell of his preaching in England and of the bishops' objection to his nonconformity, and twelve are given to the "Arguments" which Mather used to convince himself that moving to New England from Old England was "not onely lawful, but also necessary for them that are . . .

free." [36] Another six pages deal with the events of the voyage to Boston, told partly in Mather's own words copied from his journal. Obviously, for the biographer the great events of Mather's life were his making up his mind to emigrate and his journey to this country. They were great events because they had religious significance, one as an example of "vocation" and the other as an instance of God's providential protection of the devout.

As the seventeenth century advanced pious biographers realized, just as the historians did, that the New Englanders' pristine religious ardor was waning; and just as the historians tried to avert the danger by accenting the providential interpretation of history, the biographers tried also, by the same means and others, to whip up the sluggish. What better tonic for those who had fallen into a "lifeless religion" than an account of the glories which God's favor had enabled their fathers to achieve? Young men who had been born and brought up in relative security in the colonies and had never had to make sacrifices for God were fatally inclined to listlessness in their devotion to him. If anything could touch them, biography might, with its reminders of how the faithful had been rewarded and its implied threats of the punishment in store for the faithless.

The point is illustrated in the work of Increase Mather's son, Cotton, the most industrious biographer in early New England, who certainly conceived of his work as a practical service for righteousness in a day when the old virtues were too often complacently forgotten. His *Magnalia* was finished by 1697, and incorporated several "lives" that Mather had written much earlier as well as a large collection of others prepared especially for it.[37]

The whole book is a kind of jeremiad, and the biographies as well as the purely historical sections were written to rouse a lazy generation which, forgetful of God, was drifting into sin. No one was more zealous than Cotton Mather in seeking ways to restore New England's religious health. He was an assiduous preacher, but the time he spent outside of the pulpit writing history and biography is proof of his conviction that the human tradition of New England had power to waken and to convert. That tradition he read in characteristic Puritan terms, finding the best symbolization for it in the triumphs of New England's pioneer saints. To him it did not seem dead; he celebrated it in the *Magnalia* as a continuing source of vitality. To record the glories of the founding fathers and to praise them was not to pay empty honors at a tomb; it was instead to revive the pioneer saints in order that they might continue to serve as sources of life for their sons.

The biographies in the *Magnalia* are all eulogistic and didactic, but Mather manages to make some of them lively, although usually flattering and incomplete, portraits. He seems to have known a considerable number of English biographies, notably those of Thomas Fuller, which essayed to reveal character as well as deeds, and from them he learned techniques which are commonplace in biography today but were relatively novel in his time. No one of Mather's "lives" is a masterpiece; but very few indeed are wholly dull. They are partly saved from the flatness of mere eulogy by Mather's occasional introduction of rudimentary psychological analysis and of other material obviously intended to reveal the personalities and temperaments of his subjects.

There is perhaps another explanation for the fact that Mather's "lives" seem today more readable and relatively individualized and three-dimensional as compared to most Puritan biographies of the same sort written in England. His heroes were often, to a greater degree than their English counterparts, men of action, and their stories were often exciting enough to make readers forgive the didactic tone. Even though most of the men eulogized by Mather underwent generally similar experiences, colonial life offered enough variety so that Governor Winthrop, say, lived a very different sort of life from Governor Phips, and John Cotton showed his saintliness in ways unlike those of a frontier preacher or a devoted missionary like the apostle Eliot. Of course English Puritans who were made the subject of biographies also led different sorts of careers each from the other, but in general the work of a town or country parish, some sort of persecution from the Anglican authorities, or some part in Puritan politics or in the Puritan struggle for power during the Civil War were common elements in most of their lives, and elements which were neither as easy to dramatize or as inherently exciting as the adventures of a Puritan in a "howling wilderness," who had to contend with hostile Indians, physical hardships, and all the myriad problems of founding a new state. And quite apart from possibly richer material for effective narrative offered by colonial heroes, there seems to be in the early New England Puritan "lives" a greater emphasis than in the English ones on what seem today to be the most valuable moral qualities and values — the qualities and values most directly related to the needs and operations of a society — what might be described as "public" virtues. Given an English nonconformist, preaching and ministering to his flock relatively tranquilly and uneventfully, his biographer — like Samuel Clarke and Edmund Calamy, both pedestrian and diligent, and both read by New Englanders — might easily choose to center on his studiousness, his meekness, his abstemiousness of diet, his diligence in solitary prayer, or on the erudition of his sermons, and thereby produce a stereotype with little general appeal and, for most readers, little sense of life.[38] Colonial nonconformists, however, could hardly be portrayed at all except in close relation to their colleagues and neighbors in a community that felt itself united in a common quest. Inevitably therefore, Mather was likely to pick out for eulogy traits in his subjects which were useful to the society they helped to lead or were, at least, displayed in their relation to that society. Charity, public service in the pulpit or town-house, diligence in pastoral care and in education, missionary zeal — these were some of the signs of sainthood which he often chose to praise. Biographical studies of individuals who exemplified such virtues are apt to be more interesting and to seem more vivid and individual to modern readers than equally careful presentations of heroes whose lives were less bound up with the doings and fortunes of a community. The saintliness of a St. Simeon Stylites is harder to describe in moving terms than that of a St. Francis; John Eliot, "the apostle to the Indians," and William Phips, the self-made man won over to God and serving him as the governor of a colony, can be given life in the pages of a biography more easily than can a scholar working in retirement or a preacher hedged about by the relative calm of a seventeenth-century English village.

It would be dangerous to press such suggestions too far, but if they have any validity it is permissible to take one further tentative step and to suggest that some of the good qualities in early New England biography were directly related, as is so much else in other Puritan colonial literature, to the theological tenets of the colonists. Their characteristic "covenant theology" involved the idea of the Puritan community as a community, a group united by a common purpose and duty and in a specific contractual relation to God. Of course, the individual could never quite escape the burden imposed by his sense of intimate personal responsibility, but he could lighten the load by remembering that he was a member of a state or society which was collectively obligated and, provided it lived up to its covenanted obligations, assured of divine favor. One escape from

what must have been otherwise the tragic oppression of
a scheme in which men felt themselves to be essentially
evil and helpless before an avenging deity must have
been the Puritan's confidence that he was not to be
judged alone but could hope for his share in the mercy
which God might have ultimately decreed for the group
of which he was a part. A Puritan biographer who accepted the "covenant theology" might well emphasize
more than those who held different views, the "public"
aspects of his heroes' achievements and merits, and
might therefore come closer to the completeness of portraiture which is possible only when the individual is
pictured in the strong cross lighting of his relation to a
living community.

The best English biographies of the seventeenth century were by present-day standards far better than any
produced in the colonies. Izaak Walton's talent for
picturing personality by revealing just the details which
in life reveal friends to friends — for example, his
account of Bishop Sanderson in his "sad-coloured
Clothes . . . God knows, far from being costly,"
breaking off his browsing among the bookstalls to chat
with him over a pot of ale in a public house — was shared
by no one in New England and by few writers any-
where, before or since.[39] Nor were the lives written by
Mrs. Hutchinson and Richard Baxter, both Puritans,
matched in their time in the New World. Lucy Hutchinson's biography of her husband is realistic primarily
because of her characteristically Puritan homeliness of
phrase and her skill, not unlike William Bradford's, in

133

using "plain" prose to create climaxes which, given her
subject, are both more appropriate and more impressive
than any to be hoped for from a more ornate style.
Baxter's wife, whom he lovingly portrayed in his *Brevi-
ate,* was a character so fascinatingly complex that it would
have been hard to write dully of her, but he did far
more than avoid dullness, and achieved an amazingly
analytic study, probing deeply just as psychiatric inves-
tigators do today, and in choice of words and his application of them curiously anticipating theirs.[40] In both
his work and Mrs. Hutchinson's the essential impulse
and the attitude and method are those common among
Puritans. That no New Englander succeeded as they
did is not because the literary and theological principles
of colonial Puritanism prevented, but because the chance
that governs genius denied to the Mathers, John Cotton, Samuel Whiting, and Ebenezer Turell the artistic
gifts which were granted to Lucy Hutchinson and to
Baxter.[41]

Nevertheless the general literary level of New
England biographies is so high that they need no
apology. Whether one looks at England or at New
England, it is plain that there were in Puritanism
elements which contributed importantly to the evolu-
tion in the seventeenth century from the older stereotyped and formal "life" to something closer to the
modern ideal of complete portraiture of the individual.
The Puritans' vision of each man's terrifying closeness
to God, with no ecclesiastical or priestly intermediary
to hide behind, made "personal literature" precious

to them. Their work has faults and limitations, but it is full of the flavor of life, redolent of the Puritan's interest in the bases of character, and warm with the intensity of his experience. Because the core of that experience was religious, autobiographies, biographies, and even some of the diaries belong to religious literature, and a few deserve to outlive the special doctrines they illustrate. Their theology is explained and symbolized by basic realities of life and personality, and their God, although infinite and beyond man's full comprehension, is conceived of as eternally in direct relation to the joys and sufferings of the individual in a world of men.

V

"A LITTLE RECREATION OF POETRY"

I N 1726 Cotton Mather began a section in a manual
of directions for candidates for the ministry with a
statement of his attitude toward verse:

Poetry . . . has from the Beginning been in such Request,
that I must needs recommend unto you some Acquaintance with
it. Though some have had a Soul so *Unmusical*, that they have
decried all *Verse*, as being but a meer *Playing* and *Fiddling* upon
Words; All *Versifying*, as if it were more *Unnatural* than if we
should chuse *Dancing* instead of *Walking*; and *Ryme*, as if it
were but a sort of *Morisco Dancing* with *Bells*: Yet I cannot wish
you a Soul that shall be wholly *Unpoetical*. An Old *Horace* has
left us an *Art of Poetry*, which you may do well to bestow a Peru-
sal on. And besides your *Lyrick Hours*, I wish you may so far
understand an *Epic Poem*, that the Beauties of an *Homer*, and a
Virgil may be discerned with you.[1]

Then follows a warning against the bad moral
tendency of Homer, qualified, however, by the reflection,

It is especially observable, That he commonly propounds
Prayer to Heaven as a most necessary Preface unto all Important
Enterprizes . . . and he never speaks of any *Supplication* but he
brings in a Gracious Answer to it. I have seen a Travesteering
High-Flyer . . . Scoff at *Homer* for this; as making his Actors
to be like those whom the English call *Dissenters*.

Moreover, Mather points out, Homer is full of useful information about antiquities and of *"Recondite Learning,"* and offers even many "Illustrations of the *sacred Scriptures."* Virgil, too, is useful reading, although he sets up over Gods and men a "Nonsensical Power" called Fate.[2]

Cotton Mather's hopeful candidate for the ministry was not only to read poetry now and then; he might even write it:

> If . . . you try your young Wings now and then to see what Flights you can make, at least for an *Epigram*, it may a little sharpen your *Sense*, and polish your *Style*, for more important Performances . . . You may . . . all your Days, make a little *Recreation* of *Poetry* in the midst of your more painful Studies.[3]

But caution was needed:

> I cannot but advise you, *Withold thy Throat from Thirst*. Be not so set upon *Poetry*, as to be always poring on the *Passionate* and *Measured* Pages. Let not what should be *Sauce* rather than *Food* for you, Engross all your Application. Beware of a *Boundless* and *Sickly* Appetite, for the Reading of the *Poems*, which now the *Rickety* Nation swarms withal: And let not the *Circaean* Cup intoxicate you. But especially preserve the *Chastity* of your Soul from the Dangers you may incur, by a Conversation with *Muses* that are no better than *Harlots*.[4]

Ovid's epistles, for example, "excite and foment Impure *Flames*, and cast *Coals* into" the *"Bosom,"* thus deserving "to be thrown into the *Fire*." In the whole library of the powers of darkness, Mather declares, "the *Poets* have been the most *Numerous* as well as the most *Venemous*." [5]

These passages were written in the eighteenth century, but their author was all his life a champion of the standards of the older Puritanism, and what he says sums up admirably earlier Puritan attitudes toward poetry. It has a place; it can help learning; it is not mere *"Playing* and *Fiddling* upon *Words"*; and to write it may sharpen the student's *"Sense,* and polish" his *"Style."* But the style is to be polished for use in "more important Performances." Poetry is "sauce," not solid food; it is a "little *Recreation,"* not something over which an earnest man should take undue pains. Worst of all, it may kindle impure flames and so become an instrument of Satan.

Obviously no Puritan who thought thus, and apparently most of them did, was likely to give himself wholeheartedly to poetry. Nor could he draw on the full poetic resources of his time. He was trained in school and college in reading and writing Latin verse, but he had also to remember that many Latin authors were pagans whose work was to be read only for information or for bits of ethical truth. He had to be wary about some of the emotions it might stir. He lived in an age in which much great religious poetry was being written, but a large part of it smacked strongly of the doctrines, ritual, or symbolism of the Anglican or Catholic, and much of it seemed to him too sensuously evocative, dealing too boldly with material that was "Passionate" enough to kindle dangerous fires in the human breast. Above all the Puritan was handicapped as a poet because he was sure that his first duty was to

convey sound doctrine in systematic and logically comprehensible terms. However real his religious feeling
and however useful it might be to arouse others by communicating it, it was still more important that those
others should first of all understand for what end they
were aroused and should learn in as much detail as
possible what their concrete task was in daily life. They
might be piously moved by a poem; prose usually best
explained what they must do to prove their piety.

It is natural, therefore, that there is more good Puritan prose than Puritan verse. When the Puritan aspired
to poetry his flights were limited because elements in
his beliefs on religion and art which were harmless or
even useful to his prose were certainly unfriendly to
his poetry. It was not that he lacked intensity of religious feeling or that he minimized the importance of
emotions centered in God. The trouble was that the
means of giving poetic expression to the feeling were
too often denied him, either by his literary inexperience
or that of his audience, or by his separation on theological grounds from some of the best religious art of
his day. His conception of the most effective means of
carrying God's truth to fallen man tied poetry too close
to the cart of prose.

In spite of all this, New England Puritans constantly
read poetry — or at least verse — and hundreds of them
tried their hands at writing it. Anyone who explores
Puritan diaries, journals, histories, and biographies will
find in them many bits of pious rhyme. Several volumes of verse were published in Puritan New England,

and one of them enjoyed a considerable success abroad. And for every page that was printed it seems likely that several were written, to be circulated in manuscript or cherished by the author and his family. It is safe to say that the New England Puritans, far from being hostile to poetry, both needed and loved it.[6]

The reasons are plain. For one thing the seventeenth-century New England Puritan was the child of the Renaissance as well as of the Reformation. He was bred in a tradition in which poetry was an art, divinely sanctioned and powerful in the service of truth. Impious verse he hated, of course, as he did impiety in all forms, and poetry which played too much on man's sinful susceptibilities he condemned. But in Spenser and others he found proofs that the Muses could serve righteousness, and, some modern critics to the contrary, it never occurred to him to object to poetry as such. Many of his purposes could be better achieved in sermons, histories, biographies, and treatises, and a large part of his audience was able to comprehend prose better than verse, so that he put first things first and worked chiefly in prose. But this does not mean that he despised verse or that he failed to recognize that it was the most fitting style on some occasions and for some purposes. He read some classic poets; he read Spenser, he read the French poet Du Bartas as translated into English by Joshua Sylvester; he dipped into other "holy poetry" — including that of the Anglican, George Herbert — and rejoiced in what he read. Poetry was for him, as for other late-Renaissance men, both a delight and a source of truth. It was for him, as for men in all ages and all circumstances, an art which satisfied needs, not always consciously recognized or systematically theorized about, but none the less deeply felt.

Between 1712 and 1723 Joseph Tompson of Billerica, then in his seventies and early eighties, patiently copied into his journal a small sheaf of verses, written about or by older members of his family. In the midst of his arduous life as a town officer and farmer he found joy in them. He had little time to give to writing in his journal, but when it rained he used to take a few hours from his work to copy into it poems that were, he said, "memorialls and epitaphs upon my Deare." He loved "pondering & writeing and remembring afresh" his "Dear father and his Contemporaries with him." There is little doubt that it seemed appropriate to Joseph Tompson that "memorialls and epitaphs" should be in verse, and some faint stirrings of a soul "not wholly Unpoetical" must have accounted for his "soule satisfiing delight" when he read the lines he had patiently copied into his journal.[7]

There were many New Englanders like Joseph Tompson. Untutored in poetry, they were able to go no deeper into criticism than to remark, as Tompson did about one of the clumsier pieces in his collection, that it was included "not for the poetry but for the love & . . . Christian spirit breathing in" its lines.[8] Bred in a stern school, in which the hard work of daily living came first, the settlers of New England had to relegate

poetry to rainy afternoons. Thoroughly taught in
Puritan theology, they knew that the study of the Bible
and a constant effort to carry out its precepts were more
important than even the most "soule-satisfiing delight"
to be had from literature. But none the less, devout
Puritans like Tompson did get pleasure from verse,
and many of them tried their hands at making it when
what they wanted to say seemed to demand some means
of expression more impressive than prose. They were
sadly handicapped, but the impulse was there, and
New England colonial poetry is rich in suggestions for
any reader who would understand how the Puritan
thought about literature in relation to his service of
God.

Fundamental to any understanding of Puritan verse
is a realization of the extent to which its themes and
forms were dictated by its audience. Cotton Mather
was not himself a good poet, but he had read a great
deal and he had at least a rudimentary understanding
of contemporary conventions of wit and poetic style.
Of the verses of John Wilson of Boston he wrote: "If
the *curious* relished the piety sometimes rather than
the *poetry*, the capacity of the *most* therein to be accom-
modated, must be considered." [9] There could be no
clearer statement of the fact that the Puritan verse-
maker wrote not primarily to please the *"curious"* — the
sophisticated critics — but to "accomodate" "the *most*"
— to be of service to the rank and file of his readers.
Had he chosen to concentrate on artistic effect, regard-
less of whether his work would be understandable to

farmers and fishermen, he might have written better poetry, but he must often have violated fundamental articles in his literary creed. For him literature existed to move the hearts and minds of men to righteousness, and the more who understood it and were moved, the better it was. If, in order to reach more readers, some things dear to "wits" and connoisseurs had to be given up, the Puritans did not grudge the sacrifice.

A bad poem is a bad poem still, even if the reasons for its defects are understood. No amount of explaining why alters the fact that most New England Puritan poetry is inexpert in technique and flat in effect. The only reason for harping on the fact that some of the Puritan's beliefs and some of the conditions under which he worked help to account for defects in his writing, is that this is too often neglected by those who generalize about the literature of early New England. Sweeping statements about the Puritan's feeling for poetry, or his lack of it, and about the alleged incompatability of his theology with artistic expression, have often been based on a reading of a few of his poems, considered entirely without reference to the purposes for which he wrote them.

John Wilson, for example, one of the pioneer divines of Boston, published only one book of verse, *A Song of Deliverance*.[10] It has almost no poetic merit and is little more than a pedestrian rhymed chronicle of some incidents in seventeenth-century English history which Wilson thought it would be useful to record as instances of God's providential ruling of the world.

The hasty reader might easily infer from it that Wilson, renowned as a scholar and preacher in the early days of Boston, was a stranger to the Muses and was content to write only bad verse. From here it is an easy jump to the notion that Puritans, however learned, cared too little for poetry to take pains with it and were satisfied with mere rhyming. But Wilson's *Song of Deliverance* was, as its preface says, written for children. It might have been better, even for them, but its simple measures were probably pretty well adapted to the small boys and girls in Old and New England whose Puritan parents gave it to them to read as a reminder of the alarming extent of God's power. To argue to general conclusions about Puritan poetic standards on the basis of a poem specifically aimed at a children's audience would be absurd.

A second example is Michael Wigglesworth's famous *Day of Doom*, the best-seller of its day in Puritan New England, and probably "the most popular poem ever written in America." [11] It purports to picture the Judgment Day and the treatment then to be meted out to sinners and saints. Such a theme is large enough and dignified enough to demand the most spacious and solemn form, but the *Day of Doom* actually is written in ballad measure, and the trotting verses seem sadly unsuited to the subject. So Wigglesworth has been ridiculed, and his occasional flashes of real poetry forgotten, because critics have found comic or worse his use of homely stanza. Similarly, the *Day of Doom* has been attacked because much of it is merely versified theol-

ogy. The argument runs, then, that Wigglesworth was a
Puritan and a would-be poet, but so inept and so blind
to artistic values as to choose for his major work an
absurdly incongruous form and so unimaginative as to
forget the actual tragic vision of the Judgment Day
in his concern for theological detail. Therefore, it is
said, Puritan poets were inept, artistically blind, and
unimaginative. Such generalization is at the very least
dangerous if we remember that Wigglesworth, in
Cotton Mather's words, wrote verse for "the Edification of such Readers, as are for Truths dressed up in
a *Plain Meeter*." [12] The meter, however inappropriate,
was certainly plain, and it was familar to the simplest
New England reader. The purpose of the poem was
edification; therefore the more readers it reached the
better. Versified theology, if not easily adapted to the
uses of poetry, was something that everyone could read
and perhaps enjoy and remember more easily than
theology offered in sober prose. What Wigglesworth
was trying to do is as clear as his success, testified to by
the great popularity of his book. If it seems today a
poetic failure, it is worth remembering that it probably
also seemed so to Cotton Mather and to Wigglesworth
himself. They knew that the *Day of Doom* was not
aimed at literary critics but at simple folk who liked
their "Truths" and "Meeter" plain.

The classic instance usually cited to support the con-
tention that there were in Puritanism no possibilities
for poetry, and that to be a good Puritan meant to
despise it, is the *Bay Psalm Book*. [13] A translation of

the psalms probably made by Thomas Welde, John Eliot, and Richard Mather, its purpose was to provide a completely accurate metrical version for use in Puritan meetinghouses. Anyone who knows the splendid cadences of the Psalter or the 1611 Bible is unlikely to read the *Bay Psalm Book* for pleasure. "The Lord is my shepherd; I shall not want. He maketh me to lie down in green pastures; he leadeth me beside the still waters. He restoreth my soul," became in Puritan New England:

> The Lord to mee a shepheard is,
>   want therefore shall not I.
> Hee in the folds of tender-grasse,
>   doth cause mee downe to lie;
> To waters calme me gently leads
>   Restore my soule doth hee.[14]

Surely here is a clear case against the Puritans. If the Anglican and Catholic translators could make music and beauty out of the songs of David, why did the New Englanders turn them into a jumbled discord? But once again the Puritan knew what he was doing, and why. To him the text of the Psalms was important; an accurate translation was essential. If in order to be literal in his rendering he had to be harsh, he preferred exactness to smoothness. Moreover, his version of the Psalms was to be sung by Puritan congregations, which meant that it must be fitted to the tunes which New England worshippers knew. No one who has tried to set words to music, even the simplest, is likely to wonder that the authors of the *Bay Psalm Book,* who were not only fitting words to a narrow range of tunes but were forced also to give a literal rendition of a Hebrew text, fared so badly. Even the Anglican Bishop Hall, a relatively experienced and successful poet, had trouble with the problem. He defended his "metaphrase" of the Psalms, saying "Perhaps, some think the verse harsh, whose nice ear regards roundness more than sense. I embrace smoothness; but affect it not. This is the least good quality of a verse that intends any thing but musical delight." He "laboured," he said, "to keep David's entire sense with numbers neither lofty nor slubbered: which mean is so much more difficult to find, as the business is more sacred, and the liberty less." [15] The liberty of Puritan scholars was even more limited. Their reverence for the Bible forced them to regard strict fidelity as the chief virtue of any translation from it. The compilers of the *Bay Psalm Book* knew that their work was not poetry; they knew, to quote their preface, that "the verses" were "not alwayes so smooth and elegant as some" might "desire or expect." "Wee have," they wrote, "respected rather a plaine translation, then to smooth our verses with the sweetnes of any paraphrase, and soe have attended Conscience rather then Elegance, fidelity rather then poetry, in translating the hebrew words into english language, and Davids poetry into english meetre." [16] Scholarly precision and musical necessity came first; no other interest might interfere.

Such examples as have been cited show how the Puritan's audience, his determination to edify in poetry as in all other writing, and his scholarship stood in his way as a poet. The Puritan's creed, or at least the set of attitudes that he developed from it, not only tempted him to put poetry among the relative inessentials, but sometimes concretely handicapped his attempts to write it.

To grant this, however, is not to admit that the Puritan hated poetry or that he ignored it. Many a New Englander would have agreed with Richard Baxter's assertion that "there is somewhat of Heaven in Holy Poetry. It charmeth souls into loving harmony and concord." [17] New Englanders read George Herbert, in spite of his Anglicanism, because he concentrated his work on what was for the Puritan the core of religious life — the direct relation of the individual to God. Baxter said that Herbert "speaks to God like one that really believeth a God, and whose business in this world is most with God. Heart-work and Heaven-work make up his books." [18] "Heart-work and Heaven-work" were what the Puritans wanted; they knew that even if the best in their hearts and the best of Heaven was beyond the reach of words, poetry might go farther than prose or at least better suit the temper of their devotion and convey it more memorably to other men. There is no more striking instance in history of the constant need of the religious mind for some sort of poetic expression than the Puritan's quest for poetry.

Inhibited and limited as they were, inexperienced craftsmen with an inexperienced audience, they still groped for a beauty not definable in prose. As Rilke has said, poetry tries to establish "new outposts in the mystery and darkness that surround us." [19] For all the Puritan's confidence in his theology there was in his life and in his relation to God plenty of "mystery and darkness," and poetry was no mere luxury for him. It was a necessity, as it must always be for profoundly religious men, and his persistent quest of it testifies both to the depth of his feeling and the greatness of his need.

Throughout Puritan verse — excluding that which was merely metrical theologizing or plain preaching dressed up with rhyme — there is a sense of tension, arising from the conflict between the Puritan's genuine and passionate emotion and the restraints imposed by his beliefs and his environment. There is a stricter tension too, common to most religious poets, produced by his sense of the inadequacy of any finite means to express the full quality of his feeling or the full beauty of religious truth. The Puritan's theme is always in the last analysis infinite and so beyond the reach of concrete words and images. Anne Bradstreet, the first American poetess and one whose work is more imaginative and more skillful in its use of some Renaissance techniques than that of any other New England Puritan except Edward Taylor, writes, as she considers the beauty of the sun,

> Art thou so full of glory, that no Eye
> Hath strength, thy shining Rayes once to behold?
> And is thy splendid Throne erect so high
> As to approach it, can no earthly mould?

How full of glory then must thy Creator be?
Who gave this bright light luster unto thee:
Admir'd, ador'd for ever, be that Majesty.

Silent alone, where none or saw, or heard,
In pathless paths I lead my wandring feet,
My humble Eyes to lofty Skyes I rear'd,
To sing some Song my mazed Muse thought meet.
My great Creator I would magnifie,
That nature had thus decked liberally:
But Ah, and Ah, again, my imbecility!

I hear the merry grashopper then sing,
The black clad Cricket, bear a second part,
They kept one tune, and plaid on the some string,
Seeming to glory in their little Art.
Small Creatures abject, thus their voices raise?
And in their kind resound their makers praise:
Whilst I as mute, can warble forth no higher layes? [20]

Here and there in Anne Bradstreet there can be felt
also the strain set up between the essential instinctive
emotion and the bonds drawn tight against full expression by elements in the Puritan's way of thought. Her
child dies and she writes:

By nature Trees do rot when they are grown
And Plumbs and Apples thoroughly ripe do fall,
And Corn and grass are in their season mown,
And time brings down what is both strong and tall.
But plants new set to be eradicate,
And buds new blown, to have so short a date,
Is by his hand alone that guides nature and fate. [21]

She is moved by her loss and by her sense of injury
in it. She concentrates on death in maturity as inevitable

and just and finds homely images for the theme. Then her feeling for her child wells up and two lines begin to flicker toward passionate rebellion:

> But plants new set to be eradicate,
> And buds new blown to have so short a date —

but for the Puritan that way danger lay, and Anne Bradstreet, in deference to her creed, checks herself with the inept last line

> Is by his hand alone that guides nature and fate.

The best Puritan poetry usually springs from the Puritan's feeling for the beauty of the individual life and character or from his excitement in his adventures as a wayfarer toward God. Most of the memorable lines and stanzas scattered here and there through the work of many New England Puritan poets present some phase of the Puritan's personalizing and individualizing of his faith. When he turns theology into verse or paraphrases Scripture, he is usually tame; the bright flashes come only when he tries to communicate the fullness of his own experience in his hungry search for Heaven.

The best poet of Puritan New England, and one whose finest passages are memorable, is Edward Taylor. Born about 1645 in England he came to Massachusetts in 1668, graduated from Harvard, and then became minister of the frontier settlement of Westfield on the Connecticut River. There he labored until his death in 1729, "serving both as pastor and

physician to his flock," [22] and all the time writing poems.
At his death he left four hundred manuscript pages of
verse, but he instructed his heirs never to publish them.
The result was that his work remained unnoticed until
Thomas H. Johnson discovered it in the Yale Uni-
versity Library and, in 1939, edited a volume of it.

No other poet in early New England had Taylor's
talent and no other followed so closely the pattern of
the English metaphysical poets of the seventeenth century. Those poets, mostly Anglicans and not Puritans,
had built their verse on metaphor and simile, using the
figures both for their intellectual and emotional suggestions and endeavoring to convey the full sense of
an experience by the evocative power of their images.
The result was poetry which was often harsh in music
and difficult intellectually, but was at its best amazingly successful in expressing concretely religious
emotion and the ineffable values of faith. At its worst
it was only rhetorical gymnastics or an elaborately
carved but still hollow shell of hyperbole, paradox,
strained metaphor, and word-play; in the hands of
artists as imaginative as John Donne and George
Herbert it became the perfect medium for their feeling
for the divine. Donne was not popular among the
Puritans, partly no doubt because as Dean of Saint
Paul's he was a high officer in a church whose officers
they distrusted, but probably chiefly because his religious poems were too sensuously conceived, too
crowded with imagery savoring rather of this world
than of the next. George Herbert the Puritans liked

because the central note of his work was the emotion of an individual believer, dependent upon God and sincerely zealous in devotion to Him. His imagery was often drawn from Anglican forms and practices but was, compared to Donne's, restrained, and there are few of his lines that even a strict Puritan could consider dangerous in their appeal to man's vagrant passions.

Edward Taylor was not born until after Donne's death and until the type of poetry which he and Herbert wrote was largely out of fashion, but throughout his own career, lasting well into the neoclassic period of English poetry, he stuck to the forms and devices of the "metaphysical school." So did some other New Englanders before him and contemporaneous with him, but in their work the forms and devices are usually only external patterns, adopted in deference to convention. Taylor's use of the "metaphysical" metaphor and his reliance on the image combining intellectual and emotional appeal as the primary source of poetic effect, seem to represent not subservience to fashion but the choice of a poetic method integrally related to the nature of his emotion and thought. He was by no means merely an imitator, and in spite of the points of likeness between his work and Herbert's or Donne's, Taylor's poems differ essentially from theirs. The major differences stem from his Puritan beliefs. His work is not typical of New England Puritan poetry, because it is richer in insight and more expert in technique, but it is made out of characteristically Puritan elements.

He constantly emphasizes the inadequacy of poetry
to express the divine and the hopelessness of the
religious poet's task unless God's grace has been
breathed into him and his work. This note is common
in religious poetry, Puritan or not, but the Puritan gave
it special emphasis in his desire to keep clear the distinction between the essential truth which was divine and
intangible, and the concrete and finite material with
which the poet was forced to work. Taylor disparages
his own talents:

> My tatter'd Fancy; and my Ragged Rymes
>   Teem leaden Metaphors: which yet might Serve
> To hum a little, touching terrene Shines.
>   But Spirituall Life doth better fare deserve.[23]

He conceives of himself as a mere "Crumb of Earth,"
and writes:

> If it its Pen had of an Angels Quill,
>   And sharpend on a Pretious Stone ground tite,
> And dipt in Liquid Gold, and mov'de by skill,
>   In Christall leaves should golden Letters write,
>   It would but blot and blur: yea, jag and jar,
>   Unless thou mak'st the Pen and Scribener.
>
> I am this Crumb of Dust which is design'd
>   To make my Pen unto thy Praise alone,
> And my dull Phancy I would gladly grinde
>   Unto an Edge on Zion's Pretious Stone:
>   And Write in Liquid Gold upon thy Name
>   My Letters till thy glory forth doth flame.
>
> Let not th'attempts breake down my Dust I pray,
>   Nor laugh thou them to scorn, but pardon give.

Inspire this Crumb of Dust till it display
    The Glory through't: and then thy dust shall live.
Its failings then thou'lt overlook I trust,
    They being Slips slipt from thy Crumb of Dust.

Thy Crumb of Dust breaths two words from its breast;
    That thou wilt guide its pen to write aright
To Prove thou art, and that thou art the best,
    And shew thy Properties to shine most bright.
    And then thy Works will shine as flowers on Stems,
    Or as in Jewellary Shops, do jems.[24]

How can man, tied to earth, even dream of some day
joining in a heavenly chorus to praise God?

    What! I such Praises sing? How can it bee?
        Shall I in Heaven sing?
    What! I that scarce durst hope to see,
        Lord, such a thing?
      Though nothing is too hard for thee,
      One Hope hereof seems hard to mee.

    What! Can I ever tune those Melodies,
        Who have no tune at all?
    Not knowing where to stop nor Rise,
        Nor when to Fall.
      To sing thy Praise I am unfit:
      I have not learn'd my Gam-ut yet.

    But should these Praises on string'd Instruments
        Be sweetly tun'de? I finde
  I nonplust am, for no Consents
        I ever minde.
      My Tongue is neither Quill nor Bow:
      Nor can my Fingers Quavers show.

    But was it otherwise, I have no Kit:
        Which though I had, I could

> Not tune the strings, which soon would slip,
>   Though others should.
>   But should they not, I cannot play,
>   But for an F should strike an A.[25]

His ink is too muddy and his fancy too cloudy, Taylor believes, to sing fitly of spiritual beauty, unless God supplies grace. The poet is a poet only when he is actually God's instrument:

> Oh! make my heart thy Pipe: the Holy Ghost
>   The Breath that fills the same and Spiritually.
> Then play on mee, thy pipe, that is almost
>   Worn out with piping tunes of Vanity.
>   Winde musick is the best, if thou delight
>   To play the same thyselfe, upon my pipe.
>
> Hence make me, Lord, thy Golden Trumpet Choice,
>   And trumpet thou thyselfe upon the same
> Thy heart enravishing Hymns with Sweetest Voice.
>   When thou thy Trumpet soundst, thy tunes will flame.
>   My heart shall then sing forth thy praises sweet,
>   When sounded thus . . ."[26]

Although Taylor goes farther than most Puritans in his use of sensuous images, he is careful to draw a sharp line between the senses and the spirit, between what allures man carnally and what saves him from the snares of this world.

> Alas! my Soule, product of Breath Divine,
>   For to illuminate a Lump of Slime.
> Sad Providence! Must thou below thus tent
>   In such a Cote as strangles with ill s[c]ent?
>   Or in such sensuall Organs make thy stay,
>   Which from thy noble end do make thee stray?

My nobler part, why dost thou laquy to
The Carnall Whynings of my senses so?
What? thou become a Page, a Peasant! nay,
A Slave unto a Durty Clod of Clay!
Why should the Kirnell bring such Cankers forth
To please the shell, as will devour them both?
Why didst thou thus thy Milkwhite Robes defile
With Crimson spots of scarlet sins most vile?

My Muddy Tent, why hast thou done so ill
To Court and Kiss my Soule, yet kissing kill?
Why didst thou Whyning, egg her thus away,
Thy sensuall Appetite to satisfy? [27]

"Art, nature's Ape, hath many brave things done,"
Taylor says but all its achievements are

but Inventions Vents or glory:
Wits Wantonings, and Fancies frollicks plump;
Within whose maws lies buried Times, and Treasures,
Embalmed up in thick dawbd sinfull pleasures. [28]

Not even Nature, although it is God's creation, can
fully demonstrate his perfect works.

Nature doth better work than Art, yet thine
Out vie both works of nature and of Art.
Natures Perfection and the perfect shine
Of Grace attend thy deed in ev'ry part. [29]

Such passages illustrate two important qualities in
Taylor. One is his startling realism in diction and
imagery, his love for the homeliest of colloquial words
and for figures out of the most commonplace aspects of
life, in contexts where the subject seems to demand
dignity in vocabulary and image. Sometimes the effect

is merely incongruous; sometimes it makes vividly dramatic what otherwise might be tame. The second quality is Taylor's constant use of speech tone and his constant tendency toward direct discourse. His poems are usually declamations, spoken addresses, or prayers. The individual believer, the personified Soul, Satan, or even God and Christ are in Taylor less often described than made to speak for themselves. Here too the effect is sometimes incongruous and perhaps, in the case of speeches put into the mouths of God and the Saviour, shocking, but surprisingly often the utterance is moving and the dramatic quality intense.

Taylor's longest work was a poetic sequence called "Gods Determinations Touching His Elect." It is the story, told in a series of poems, of God's choosing some men to salvation, of the conflicts the elect go through in order to achieve assurance through faith, and of the mercy shown to them. The subject is characteristic of the Puritan, one more variant on his central theme of the individual pilgrim's progress toward God. But the treatment is not that of the formal theologian. The ideas are dramatized; the whole structure is that of drama. Justice and Mercy argue in a long dialogue about the best treatment of man. Then comes a narrative interlude of four poems on man's perplexity when called to account for his sins, God's love in selecting those to be saved, the intransigence of the chosen in the face of God's decree, and Satan's fury at their escape from his grasp. The terror of fallen Adam, the archetype for unredeemed man, is presented vividly:

He on his skirts with Guilt and Filth out peeps,
With Pallid Pannick Fear upon his Cheeks,
With Trembling joynts, and Quivering Lips, doth quake,
As if each word he was about to make
Should hackt assunder be, and Chopt as small
As Potherbs for the pot . . .
His Spirits are so low they'l scarce afford
Him Winde enough to wast a single word
Over the Tongue unto one's eare: yet loe,
This tale at last with sobs and sighs lets goe:
Saying, "my Mate procur'de me all this hurt,
Who threw me in my best Cloaths in the Dirt." [30]

Here is for the moment the cowardly husband of any New England village, blaming his wife for his plight. When, in the next poem, God decides to save men, Taylor dramatizes it by having "a Royall Coach" with a "scarlet Canopy" on "silver Pillars," and with a floor of gold, sent for the elect.[31] Their reluctance to renounce their sinful ways is displayed in a battle scene:

. . . Mercy persues apace,
Then some Cast down their arms, Cry Quarter, Grace!
Some Chased out of breath, drop down with feare,
Perceiving the persuer drawing neer.
The rest persude, divide into two rancks,
And this way one, and that the other prancks.

Then in comes Justice with her forces by her,
And doth persue as hot as sparkling fire.
The right wing then begins to fly away:
But in the streights strong Baracadoes lay.
They're therefore forc'd to face about, and have
Their spirits Quel'd, and therefore Quarter Crave.[32]

Some New England Puritans had seen royal coaches in London and they all had at least read of them; they knew all there was to know about cowardly husbands and angry soldiers. Taylor, in characteristically Puritan fashion, is clothing doctrine in images drawn from familiar objects and events.

The next poem in the sequence is an address of the tormented soul to Christ, its "Honour'd Generall," and this is followed by Christ's speech in reply. After another short narrative interlude comes a long dialogue between Satan and the Soul, and all but four or five of the other poems in "Gods Determinations" are speeches of Satan, the Soul, Christ, or God, or dialogues between characters in the divine drama. The remaining verses are lyric outbursts commenting on, and marveling at, what to the poet is the beauty of the wayfaring soul's search for blessedness and God's mercy to it. In its structure, then, "Gods Determinations" is essentially a play, with a kind of chorus which comments on the action or explains parts of it in dramatic narrative.[33]

A good example of Taylor's skill in capturing the effect of colloquial and earthy speech is Satan's opening speech in his dialogue with the Soul. He ridicules the elect, insisting that their conversion cannot last and that they have left him for trifling rewards. They are like dogs answering a whistle:

> Soon ripe, soon rot. Young Saint, Old Divell. Loe!
> Why to an Empty Whistle did you goe?
> What! Come Uncall'd? And Run Unsent for? Stay,
> It's Childrens Bread. Hands off: out, Dogs, away.

To this the Soul replies:

> It's not an Empty Whistle: yet withall,
> And if it be a Whistle, then a Call:
> A Call to Childrens Bread, which take we may.
> Thou onely art the Dog whipt hence away.[34]

The movement and tone of both speeches is admirably contrived for purposes of characterization. Satan's is staccato and harsh — the speech of an angry man, using phrases like whips. The Soul replies more calmly, in smoother cadences, and the effect is of gentleness opposed to rage.

Even more striking is Christ's reply to the anguished soul, which has cried for aid. The first four stanzas are in their diction and phrasing nothing but a Puritan lullaby or love song couched in just such language as Puritan fathers and mothers must often have used to console frightened children, or lovers to comfort each other.

> Peace, Peace, my Hony, do not Cry,
> My Little Darling, wipe thine eye,
>   Oh Cheer, Cheer up, come see.
> Is anything too deare, my Dove,
> Is anything too good, my Love,
>   To get or give for thee?
>
> If in the severall thou art,
> This Yelper fierce will at thee bark:
>   That thou art mine this shows.
> As Spot barks back the sheep again,
> Before they to the Pound are ta'ne,
>   So he, and hence 'way goes.

But if this Cur that bayghs so sore,
Is broken tootht, and muzzled sure,
   Fear not, my Pritty Heart.
His barking is to make thee Cling
Close underneath thy Saviours wing.
   Why did my sweeten start?

And if he run an inch too fur,
I'le Check his Chain, and rate the Cur,
   My Chick, keep close to mee.
The Poles shall sooner kiss and greet,
And Paralells shall sooner meet,
   Than thou shall harmed bee.[35]

Except for the last three lines about the poles and about parallels which come perhaps from Taylor's reading of Donne, these verses are keyed to the simple emotions and simple language of simple folk. However startling it may be to have Christ call the soul by pet names, or refer to the ways of sheep-dogs, or use New England dialect, Taylor's lines convey poignantly the honesty and warmth of a genuine religious emotion. Few poetic treatments of the same theme, however dignified their language and imagery, are more moving than his.

Apart from "Gods Determinations," most of Taylor's best work was done in a long series of "Sacramental Meditations," each written on the occasion of a celebration of the sacrament of the Eucharist. They were, in Taylor's own words, "Preparatory Meditations before my Approach to the Lords Supper," [36] and most of them were related to Biblical texts. Ninety-seven of the texts are from the Old Testament, and of these seventy-six come from the Song of Solomon. One hundred and twenty-four texts were drawn from the New Testament, and of these more came from the Gospel of John than from any other book.[37] The central theme of all the "Meditations" is love — the love felt for Christ by man who had been redeemed by his sacrifice.

Upon that sacrifice rested the Puritan's hope of Heaven. God and Adam had agreed together that if Adam was obedient he and his descendants should be granted happiness for all time. Adam broke the contract by disobeying and thereby doomed all men to torment. But Christ suffered to redeem mankind, and God, in his mercy, made a new covenant under which the elect — those who were given grace and could truly believe — were promised the joys of eternal life. The cardinal test of election was faith, and a loving and humble recognition of the Lord's Supper as a way of honoring the memory of Christ's death and resurrection was a proof of faith. The sacrament could not make Christians, but it was a means toward conversion. It was a concrete symbol of God's infinite goodness, a reminder of man's fall through Adam's sin and of God's new covenant with the world. The more devout the believer, the more lovingly he regarded it.

Cotton Mather declared, "The Lords Supper is a *Love-Feast*, and we should have a *Love-fire* at it." And Samuel Willard, systematically expounding Puritan theology, wrote:

This Ordinance is called a Feast, and Feasts are made for friendship, which supposeth love . . . It is to be a Commemoration of the greatest love, which cannot be done as it ought to be,

without the reciprocation of our most ardent and intense Love
. . . If we love Christ as we ought, he is our all . . . If we do
not come to enjoy him, and lie in his Embraces, we do not
come with a right design, nor can we expect to profit.[38]

It is the "ardent and intense love" of which Willard
writes that makes the major theme of Taylor's "Meditations," but what is cool in Willard is warmed by Taylor's emotion. His poems were his "Love-fires" and
he does not explain doctrine as Willard does, but
objectifies it in the sensuous and the concrete. The first
"Meditation" sets the tone for most of them:

> Oh, Matchless Love! Filling Heaven to the brim!
>   O'rerunning it: all running o're beside
> This World! Nay, Overflowing Hell, wherein
>   For thine Elect, there rose a mighty Tide!
>   That there our Veans might through thy Person bleed,
>   To quench those flames, that else would on us feed.
>
> Oh! that thy love might overflow my Heart!
>   To fire the same with Love: for Love I would.
> But oh! my streight'ned Breast! my Lifeless Sparke!
>   My Fireless Flame! What Chilly Love, and Cold?
>   In measure small! In Manner Chilly! See!
>   Lord, blow the Coal: Thy Love Enflame in mee.[39]

Two passages from other "Meditations" show how close
Taylor came to the song of earthly passion in his effort
to express the quality of his love for the divine:

> Shall I not smell thy sweet, oh! Sharons Rose?
>   Shall not mine Eye salute thy Beauty? Why?
> Shall thy sweet leaves their Beautious sweets upclose?
>   As halfe ashamde my sight should on them ly?

My Lovely One, I fain would love thee much,
　　But all my Love is none at all I see;
Oh! let thy Beauty give a glorious t[o]uch
Upon my Heart, and melt to Love all mee.
Lord, melt me all up into Love for thee,
Whose Loveliness excells what love can bee.[40]

Taylor's love is coupled with humility. In the thirty-
eighth "Meditation," which is developed through a
whole series of legal images — entirely appropriate to
the Puritan conception of the covenant of grace as essentially a legal contract between God and man — the last
verse is:

My Case is bad. Lord, be my Advocate.
　My sin is red: I'me under Gods Arrest.
Thou hast the Hit of Pleading; plead my state.
Although it's bad, thy Plea will make it best.
If thou wilt plead my Case before the King,
I'le Waggon Loads of Love and Glory bring.[41]

Here is Taylor's love for the speech tone; here in
the "Hit of Pleading" and the "Waggon Loads of
Love" is his talent for the poignantly simple phrase;
and here, certainly, in the image of Man arrested by
God, feeling his guilt, and calling on Christ as a lawyer
to plead for him, is a striking dramatization of the concept of man's necessary humility before the divine
tribunal.

The imagery of the "Meditations" is throughout
warmer, more sensuous, and more sharply pictorial

166

than that of most Puritan poetry. There is a bird of Paradise, there are roses and other flowers, and jewels. There is Taylor's "Kit" — his little violin — and other musical images; there is a special emphasis on perfumes; and there is, in one case, even incense in a censer. For most of this there is Biblical precedent, but Taylor's tendency, as his devotion to The Song of Solomon reveals, is to select the metaphors and similes which have most direct sensuous appeal. The suggestion is that although he was an orthodox Puritan, he felt as a poet a sense of constraint within the bounds of the ordinary plainness and sobriety of Puritan literary style. No one knows why he asked his heirs not to publish his verses, but he may well have felt that in some of them his passionate expression, his delight in color and fragrance, and his sometimes erotically suggestive imagery would offend his graver colleagues. It is probable, too, that he knew that his work, in its more complex passages, would only puzzle the poetically inexpert Puritan audience.

What would a strictly orthodox and unimaginative New Englander have made of such a poem as this one, on a "Sweeping Flood" which overtook New England in 1683?

> O! that I'd had a tear to've quencht that flame
> Which did dissolve the Heavens above
> Into those liquid drops that came
> To drown our carnal love.
> Our cheeks were dry and eyes refusde to weep.
> Tears bursting out ran down the skies darke cheek.

Were th'Heavens sick? must wee their Doctors bee
And Physick them with pills, our sin?
To make them purge and vomit; see:
And Excrements out fling?
We've griev'd them by such Physick that they shed
Their Excrements upon our lofty heads.[42]

Even if "carnal love" be construed as referring not to
a sexual experience but simply to the proneness of men to
fix their affections on this world rather than the next,
the immediate impression of the phrase would still be
for many readers erotic. Even though the doctrine of
the poem is unexceptionable — man so grieves God by
his sin and his failure to repent that the very skies are
purged and defile the defiant sinner — a reader untutored in the ways of "metaphysical" poetry might well
have trouble in discovering what the verses meant.
And even though moral meaning were clear and the
central situation conceived of as sexually innocent, it
would still be hard to avoid feeling in the whole poem,
with its "tortuous language, reflecting the violence of
the mood," [43] rather an assertion of hopeless and unre-
pentant guilt than an assertion of man's duty to be
humble before God. It is small wonder that Taylor
chose never to publish these lines.

Furthermore, although it is no doubt literally true,
as his editor remarks,[44] that Taylor nowhere makes the
Sacrament into a rite mystically efficacious in itself, it is
also true that the tone of his lyric adoration in many
verses certainly evokes an emotion close to that felt by
those Christians who regarded the Lord's Supper not

simply as a commemorative rite, graced by the spiritual presence of Christ, but as a chance for the believer to achieve something like direct physical union with Him by actually eating and drinking His flesh and blood. Such an idea Taylor would have denied, no doubt, in good Puritan fashion, but hot poetic emotion cannot always be kept within the limits of reasoned doctrine and may demand expression in forms which its author, in his less ecstatic moods, would reject.

Taylor's poems reveal both the defects and the virtues of the Puritan's literary creed when applied to poetry. His drastically realistic colloquialisms, his constant use of imagery drawn from the most commonplace activities of everyday life — for example, his poem beginning "Make me, O Lord, thy Spin[n]ing Wheele compleat" [45] in which the whole operation of spinning yarn and weaving the cloth becomes an extended metaphor for man's spiritual progress — and his use of events, characters, phrases, and images from the Bible, show the Puritan's reasoned belief in plain language, in material comprehensible to the Puritan audience, and in the supreme authority of Holy Writ. Taylor proves that this belief need not keep a truly gifted artist from writing good, or even great, poetry. On the other hand, his consistent selection of the Biblical imagery richest in color and in sensuous or even erotic effect, and his use in the "Meditations" of the Song of Solomon more often than any other book of the Bible, suggest that as a poet he unconsciously moved away from the relative asceticism of the Puritan toward the Catholic acceptance of the role of the senses in worship. So also the complication and obscurity of some of his verse indicate a rebellion of sorts against the cardinal Puritan doctrine of clarity in expression, a rebellion dictated by a feeling that the fundamental spiritual verities were too mysterious for logical or prosaic exposition and demanded instead all the rich emotional and intellectual suggestiveness of complex "metaphysical" poetry. When he stays on the level of straightforward theological reasoning of the sort so common in Puritan writing, Taylor is tame and often awkward; when the "quick Passions," which his grandson said he possessed,[46] took command, he became a poet.

The Puritans' loving humility before God, their vision of spiritual beauty, the grandeur of their conception of the divine, and the glory they felt was represented by their individual and collective services as soldiers and pilgrims of Christ, were themes fit for poetry. Taylor made good use of them. The substance of his work is the way of life and the faith of Puritan New England; his poetic method is the expression of his conviction that faith and life were one and that neither the spiritual nor the material had meaning except when they were united. In his finest lines, the union is achieved. Doctrine takes on life and the reader is warmed by the central fire of Puritan piety.

"Gods Determinations" begins with a "Preface," which, in the first fourteen lines rises to a climax:

> Infinity, when all things it beheld,
> In Nothing, and of Nothing all did build,

Upon what Base was fixt the Lath, wherein
He turn'd this Globe, and riggalld it so trim?
Who blew the Bellows of his Furnace Vast?
Or held the Mould wherein the world was Cast?
Who laid its Corner Stone? Or whose Command?
Where stand the Pillars upon which it stands?
Who Lac'de and Fillitted the earth so fine,
With Rivers like green Ribbons Smaragdine?
Who made the Sea's its Selvedge, and it locks
Like a Quilt Ball within a Silver Box?
Who Spread its Canopy? Or Curtains Spun?
Who in this Bowling Alley bowld the Sun? [47]

The concept of creation as the work of a skillful craftsman is trite enough, but the vividness of Taylor's
emerald green rivers lacing the earth, or his "Quilt Ball
within a Silver Box," is the hallmark of his special skill.
And the last line, "Who in this Bowling Alley bowld
the Sun," has the imaginative strength of great poetry.
Taylor's God was not content to fix the sun on its orbit
in the firmament; he must, with a magnificent sweep of
the arm, bowl it into place. The image makes him
just what Taylor felt him to be — a God so great, so
serenely powerful, that even the sun is for him a toy,
a bowling ball, and all the material wonders of the universe are merely the appurtenances of a bowling green.
The metaphor is dynamic not static; it calls up a whole
complex of intellectual and emotional responses, centered on a majestic conception of God. That conception
was the glowing heart of Puritanism. Most Puritan
poets cherished the coal but could rarely blow it to a
flame. Taylor's imagination and Taylor's skill fanned

it to a blaze of poetry and proved, if proof were needed, that deep within Puritanism, as within every living religious movement, there were values that only the artist could express.

VI

THE PURITAN LEGACY

For at least a century after the landing at Plymouth the intellectual life of the New England colonies was dominated by Puritan thought. Churches and schools followed the old patterns, and the leaders in all walks of life were at least professedly loyal to the teachings of the founding fathers. It is reasonable to suppose, therefore, that the prejudices and mental habits of the colonists must have affected somehow the behavior and attitudes of later New Englanders, and more than one critic has detected in present-day New England signs of its Puritan inheritance. The matter is of more than local interest, since men from Massachusetts and Connecticut and Rhode Island followed the advancing frontier. Some of their ideas and standards took root and flourished far west of the Hudson, and it is pretty generally admitted that somewhere in America's total cultural heritage and the complex of qualities which make up the "American character" there are traces of Puritanism.

It is very difficult, however, to be sure just what these traces are, partly because the continuing influence in intellectual history of any past "state of mind" is always hard to assess, and partly because the special "state of mind" of the New England colonists has been often misunderstood or falsely defined. The very words "Puritan" and "Puritanism" have been given so many different interpretations that they have almost lost meaning. Some critics have operated on the simple principle of calling Puritan any idea or mode of behavior of which they disapprove; others, just as emotional and no less mistaken, have been run away with by enthusiasm for the colonists' virtues and have ascribed most of the good in contemporary American civilization to the beneficent influence of the first settlers of Massachusetts Bay. The religious fundamentalist and the reactionary are still dubbed Puritans, but so, now and then, are liberals. Prohibition was glibly called a product of Puritanism, though the Puritans themselves never dreamed of a world without spirits, ale, and wine. Book censorship is decried as a survival of Puritanism by those who forget that the Puritans allowed the importation and circulation of books which in recent years have been banned here or there in this country or forbidden to enter it. Emerson and Hawthorne have been called Puritans, but so have men who disagreed with them at almost every point. Joseph Lee, in a letter to the *Boston Herald,* once summed up the confusion by writing:

The case against the Puritans is conclusive. We of the present generation have two kinds of faults; puritanical and otherwise — especially otherwise. The former are clearly a direct inheritance from the Puritans, the latter a reaction against them. Both kinds are thus the faults of the Puritans and of no one else. We ourselves, accordingly, have no faults. This is what we have always felt, but it has never been so clearly proved before.[1]

Part of the confusion comes from the fact that colonial Puritanism was not static, but changed its character radically in the space of relatively few years. The earlier chapters of this book have dealt principally with what might be called its "original" or "pioneer" phase as a radical reform movement conducted by a group of devout Protestants who dissented from the practices of the English church and became leaders of a crusade for a new state and a new church which should put into effect the will of God as revealed in Holy Writ. But in New England the "movement of dissent" changed to "an institution with authority." [2] The essentials of the formal theology and the polity persisted and hardened into a system. From the second stage of Puritanism — crystallized in a conservative and dominant church, the more rigid in its tenets the more it was threatened by new doctrines — stem most of the stiff intolerance of mind, the sterile reverence for rule as rule, the moral oppressiveness, the deference to a tradition become lifeless and bleak, which hostile critics confidently point out as marks of the Puritan heritage.

The later Puritans in New England were essentially conformists, the earlier were thorough-going nonconformists. The distinction is of great importance. It has been said that all men in all times can be divided into conformists and nonconformists, into those who reverence tradition, submerge the individual in the organization, and set form in religion above life, and those for whom man's own relation to God is the center, and individual inquiry and conviction, not corporate dogma, is the key to truth.[3] According to this hypothesis the "original" Puritans represent the second class. It is their bequest to the future which principally concerns the intellectual historian who seeks in colonial New England for the source of a fruitful tradition.

In considering the ways in which the ideals and methods of the Puritan literary artist — or would-be artist — affected later writing and later criticism, it is important to differentiate between the pioneers of colonial New England and their more complacently orthodox successors. Such men as Shepard, Wigglesworth, Norton, Roger Williams, or the testy Nathaniel Ward, the "simple cobbler" of Ipswich, wrote with a saltiness, a homely directness, and a realism grounded in their intense conviction that anything from a mouse nibbling a book to a disastrous fire or an eclipse symbolized the relentless but ultimately benevolent reign of God. They wrote of sin, of death, of divine love, and of the miraculous stirrings of grace in the hearts of the regenerate, not as a literary exercise or a polite gesture of empty conformity but with the full fervor of passionate faith in a theology and in the grandeur and beauty of the God which it exalted. But many of their sons and grandsons lost the authentic accent because they had lost the authentic faith and had substituted for the excitements of a perilous personal quest for salvation the tamer satisfactions of a decorous acceptance of a creed and polity sanctioned rather by convention than conviction.

Others, of course, were as earnestly devout as their forefathers and wrote with something of the old stylistic energy, but even in their pages the "plain style" tends to become both plainer and more dull. They wrote for men who could no longer respond as directly as the first settlers to the presentation of simple objects of daily life as symbols of the divine and whose tastes in literature turned more and more to the placid urbanities of the sermons and essays of Queen Anne's London. "The man of Locke," Emerson said, "is virtuous without enthusiasm, and intelligent without poetry," [4] and so were many — perhaps most — New Englanders in the early eighteenth century. They could not catch the full flavor of earlier Puritan prose, and inevitably those who preached and wrote for them had to shift their stylistic ground. For Emerson, Franklin was the type of the American become "frugal, inoffensive," and "thrifty," with "nothing heroic" in him.[5] Certainly, many of Franklin's compatriots were no longer stirred by the old heroic conception of the Christian pilgrimage or by vision of this world as real only in its immediate relation to Heaven and Hell, Satan and God.

"The man of Locke" and "Franklin's man" accepted cheerfully no doubt Mather Byles's linking an excerpt from "the correct, the delicate, the sublime *Addison*" with a passage from the Psalms, as comparable examples of grandeur of imagery and "Pomp of Eloquence." Byles's grandfather and great-grandfather, Richard and

Increase Mather, would have felt it impious to couple the Psalmist with any "profane" author, however "correct" or "sublime." [6] To them it would have seemed that Byles in his preaching preferred the sauce of rhetorical elegance to the solid meat of truth. They could write the "plain style" because the character of their audience enabled them "by a simple reference, to place all the meaning and force of a Bible universe behind a point." [7] But Byles had too often to strain for stylistic effect if he was to please his fashionable and complacent eighteenth-century andience in a Boston that was losing its character as the center of a Bible commonwealth and becoming a worldly, if provincial, metropolis. The old convictions were weakening, the old symbols were losing their power, and too often the preacher of Byles's time tried to compensate by the exaggerated artifices or downright sentimentality of a "melting" style. Preaching on Philippians 3: 21, in 1732, Byles expatiates on the phrase "our vile body" in a way that would have been impossible for his pioneer forebears.

Is this the Face we once gaz'd upon with so much Pleasure? Are these the Cheeks that glow'd so fresh, and bloom'd so lovely? Are these the Lips that smil'd so graceful, and pour'd out such a gliding Stream of Eloquence and Musick? Where's the tuneful Voice that once held the listening Ear, and rais'd the attentive Eye? Where are the proportioned Limbs, the supple Joints, the vigorous Pulses, the beating Heart, the working Brain, and the breathing Breast? Lo, the Body is laid in the Dust, and the Worms cover it. Polluted Vermine crawl over every Part of the elegant Form, and the beautious Face. It is folded in a winding Sheet, it is nailed in a black Coffin, and it is deposited in a silent

Vault, amidst Shades and Solitude. The Skin breaks and moulders away; the Flesh drops in Dust from the Bones; the Bones are covered with black Mould, and Worms twist about them. The Coffins break, and the Graves sink in, and the disjointed Skelliton strows the lonely Vault. This shapely Fabrick must leave its Ruins among the Graves; lie neglected and forgot; moulder away without a Name, and scatter among the Elements. "And were these Bones once living like ours? and must ours be as they"? This hideous Skull, the frightful Jaw fallen, and the black Teeth naked to the Eye, was it once a thinking Frame, covered with a beauteous Skin? Strange Alteration made by Death! [8]

The rhetoric is skillful, but its effect is that of sentimental hyperbole. Fresh cheeks and blooming lips, "proportioned Limbs," and an "elegant Form" and "beautious Face" no doubt pleased Byles's hearers as a theatrical performance might, but their emotional response to his picture of the horrors of death can hardly have involved more than a pleasant shudder or a complacent tear or two.

Byles had genuine literary gifts and a facile wit, but all too often his prose, like that of some of his other contemporaries, rings hollow when it treats the central Puritan issues. It is moulded not by an all-consuming interest in those issues or by respect for the literary canons of earlier New England, but by a modish conformity to the manner of the polite English essayists of Byles's day. Those essayists influenced many American men of letters, but they have nothing to do with a literary inheritance from Puritanism. For that one must go back to the days when colonial Puritanism was both a "state of mind" and a way of life and when its writers chose their methods with less regard for literary fashions than for the immediate communication of what they held to be divine truth to an audience eager for that truth and responsive to the fundamental symbolism of Puritan literature which for them expressed the central verities.

The "plain style" of the early Puritans was a tangible influence on one of the most striking stylistic phenomena of the seventeenth century, the movement toward "plainness" in prose. By 1700 many writers were judging the merit of prose by its clarity, its relative simplicity of diction and structure, by its avoidance of the elaborately figurative, and by the extent to which it was, in the parlance of the day, "natural and unaffected." The theory that the passions and the reason were in opposition and that, in general, the passions led to error and reason to truth was related to the notion that metaphors and the adornments of prose served passion — and therefore error — rather than reason and truth. The tendency was to standardize prose style. This limited the range of its movement and the variety of its texture but turned it none the less into an admirable instrument for an age increasingly concerned with logic and reason, scientific and mathematical method, as the essential forms for thought.

There is no question that Puritan theories helped to produce the new prose. Puritanism, whatever its defects, was a movement that brought to thousands of Englishmen a new excitement in books, sermons, and especially in the Bible. Its strength rested on its appeal to a great class which was for many years not only to control English politics but to fix its ways of life and standards of taste as norms for the larger part of the nation. This class, the Puritan audience, was both in England and the colonies made up of men and women who were neither sensitive literary critics nor capable of appreciating the most sophisticated and "witty" writing of their time, but generally speaking wanted books to be "useful" and could find no "use" in highly recondite allusions, complex rhetoric, or imaginative flights beyond the reach of sober hard-working English folk. Such readers demanded that their sermons and books be intelligible first of all, and their emotional response to what they heard and read was greatest when the author spoke the language of everyday life. Throughout the seventeenth century, religious books and especially printed sermons were among the most popular works of the day, if not the most popular, and for a large part of the period these works were commonly directed to an audience of Puritans, or, in the later decades, of men who if not Puritan in the strict sense had absorbed Puritan theories about the usefulness of pious literature and the vanity of writing that could not readily be understood by simple people. Inevitably preachers and pious writers used the "plain style," and a great part of the nation became habituated through sermons and religious books to the orderly clarity of Puritan texts.

In New as well as in Old England the "plain style" held sway long after the days of the original Puritans.

A few men, like Cotton Mather, reverted in part of their work at least to more elaborate conventions of prose, but in general from 1700 on the basic principles of the Puritan style appear in much of the best American writing. In preaching especially a long line of modern practitioners have reiterated as fundamental to their art many of the rules emphasized by the early New England divines. The Puritans developed those rules from tradition and from their experience; apparently the tradition is still valid and still empirically confirmed. The authors of the long series of Lyman Beecher Lectures on Preaching, given at Yale University for a period of seventy-seven years, have stuck pretty consistently to precepts which any Puritan would have approved, and John Brown, who gave the lectures in 1899-1900, chose to center them about "Puritan preaching in England." [9] In his work and that of his colleagues there are exhortations to students of preaching to try for "clearness" and "concreteness" and to avoid "sensationalism" and, at least in excess, "elegance." [10] There are repetitions of the typical Puritan idea that "a good style, written or spoken, is like a pane of clear glass" while "a bad or 'eloquent' style is like a stained-glass window." Shades of Anglican George Herbert and Puritan Richard Baxter! [11] The Yale lecturers also insist that the preacher's "chief concern is with the message, but the message ought not to be handicapped by a bad style," which is one lacking in clearness, concreteness, and unity.[12] "Illustrations" are useful but must not be abused or overused, and apparently abuse and overuse are very like what the Puritan meant when he inveighed against dangerous appeals to the senses and ornamentation of style for the sake of merely literary effect. As for diction, words "must be chosen with care . . . the language must be simple, clear, and accurate. If it can also be beautiful that is an added virtue." [13] To all this most Puritan preachers would have contentedly cried "Amen!"

Fortunately, in the sermon as well as in other types of writing more than mere "plainness" has survived as a stylistic legacy from the Puritans. Franklin's talent for vivid phrasing and his taste for earthy images certainly came in part from the New England of his youth. Jonathan Edwards' success in expounding his impressive and complex philosophy was made possible because he had learned to write with transparent clarity and to enlist simple phrasing and restrained diction in the service of beauty. Ralph Waldo Emerson was a master of the homely image and reverted to a familiar figure when he said of Carlyle's rhetoric, which he disliked, "The merit of glass is not to be seen, but to be seen through, but every crystal and lamina of the Carlyle glass shows." [14] James Russell Lowell did not much like Henry Thoreau, but he thought his metaphors and images were good because they were "always fresh from the soil." [15] Thoreau himself delighted in the "strong, coarse, homely speech" of "some of the early writers of New England" because it "brings you very near the thing itself described. The strong new soil speaks through them . . . That generation stood nearer to nature, nearer to the facts, than this, and hence their books have more life in them." [16]

It was the strength, the homeliness, the "life" of early colonial Puritan writing which did most for a few later literary artists in this country, not its mere simplicity and logical clarity which, however influential in their effect on the course of English style, often lent themselves after 1700 to prose both flat and dull. The strength, the homeliness, and the "life" came from the organic relation of Puritan style to Puritan concepts in the days when to be a Puritan was to be a pilgrim, a warrior, or even a tragic hero in a universal drama. The point is not that the later American artist has consciously chosen the New England colonists as literary masters, but that at times certain of their stylistic habits fixed in New England books and speech have served him well when moral or religious issues have stirred him to an ardor comparable to theirs.

A similar line of influence may be traced from the Puritan's interest in biography written with an emphasis on the portrayal of character rather than on mere events. They accented the "inner life" and in so doing helped to develop and popularize new techniques for analyzing and depicting character. It is reasonable to suppose that American biography since colonial days has matured more rapidly than it could have if the Puritan colonists and their sympathizers abroad had not written lives with zeal and skill. Certainly in another kind of "personal literature" New Englanders have followed in the footsteps of the founding fathers.

The habit of writing diaries and autobiographies persisted for generations in New England, and no doubt still persists. What is *The Education of Henry Adams* essentially but a somewhat more sophisticated and somewhat less frank variant of the analysis which the Puritan practiced in his diary or autobiography? Any reader who turns from Puritan "personal literature" to it or to the journals of Emerson or Thoreau or Hawthorne recognizes that there is a link between nineteenth-century New England and the New England of the Puritans.

As for history, the case is plainer still. Cotton Mather's *Magnalia* was followed in 1736 by Thomas Prince's incomplete history of New England, which for all its faults had some major historical virtues. Prince declared: "I cite my *Vouchers* to every Passage: And I have done my utmost first to find out the *Truth*, and then to relate it in the clearest Order." [17] A recent historian, John Spencer Bassett, comments: "Posterity is willing to grant that he achieved his object, and it gives him a place among the most worthy of our historical scholars." [18] The relation between the early Puritan's respect for accurate recording and Prince's insistence on "finding out the truth" is plain. So is the relation between Puritan historical standards and those of Thomas Hutchinson, "probably the best historian who wrote in the colonial period," whose history of Massachusetts began publication in 1764.[19] Mr. Bassett says that Hutchinson's work "is broad and well balanced, details are subordinated to larger movements," and in it Hutchinson's task of creating, "as a liberal and able man of culture . . . a picture of the colony's progress," is "performed . . . in the manner of a master." [20]

The tradition of historical writing in, and about, New England is a long and distinguished one. English critics in the days when they were just becoming conscious of the United States as a nation must have been startled to discover that however barbarous they might wish to consider this land to be, some of its historians showed maturity and skill worthy of the Old World. Wherever history is studied today the names of Motley, Prescott, and Parkman are remembered; Jeremy Belknap, Jared Sparks, George Bancroft, and a dozen other New Englanders are not so often recalled to mind nowadays, but they all partook of New England's enthusiasm for history and each of them contributed to its historical productivity and to its progress in the effective use of the best historical techniques.

The Puritans do not deserve all the credit and other districts than New England produced good histories. In quantity and quality, however, the successors of the Puritans achieved more than any other American group, and although they learned from German scholars or from other critics of, and practitioners in, historiography, it is hard to resist the conclusion that one reason for their achievement was that the local tradition gave importance to history and supported a high standard for it.

It is true that later historians abandoned one of the

essential elements in the Puritan's historical attitude. He interpreted history as the revelation of God's providence, but late seventeenth- and eighteenth-century thinkers pushed God off into the position of a mere first cause. As science increasingly asserted its own ability to account for all phenomena, the role of the Almighty in history became less and less important. The historian rowed with the intellectual current and relaxed the Puritan's concentration on the providential interpretation.

Yet it is possible to trace the spirit of the Puritan's reading of history, although not its letter, among his descendants in days when his theology no longer prevailed. Is not the New England historian's liking for the history which sharply contrasts right and wrong, heroic and base, and looks on a specific series of happenings as part of a larger heroic progress, a liking which is closely akin to the Puritan's attitude? Bancroft, writing a history of this country, was "impressed . . . with . . . the grandeur and vastness of the subject." [21] It had grandeur because "the United States constitute an essential portion of a great political system, embracing all the civilized nations of the earth. At a period when the force of moral opinion is rapidly increasing they have the precedence in the practice and defence of the equal rights of man." [22] This confidence that the United States "were far ahead of all the other nations of the world" is very close to the Puritan's firm belief that he belonged to a people especially chosen by God.[23] Motley's "honest love for all which is good and admirable in human character wherever he finds it, while he unaffectedly hates oppression, and . . . selfishness" smacks of the Puritan's desire to demonstrate through history the superiority of the godly and to prove that the story of mankind was one of continuous warfare between good and evil.[24] Motley "hated the absolute government of the Spanish monarchy, he disliked the dogmas of the Roman church, and he could not abide the repressive spirit of the Roman hierarchy." "His histories were Protestant," certainly, in their anti-Catholicism; they were Protestant, too, and Puritan, in their insistence on a moral interpretation of character and event.[25] Parkman, the greatest of all New England historians and the one who in his personal character seems most like what we imagine the conventionally austere Puritan to have been, is a historian perhaps least like the Puritan in that he wrote with much less emphasis on religious issues. But he did share the Puritan's faith in the importance of history and a determination to pursue accuracy and truth at all costs. Moreover, the heroes Parkman most admired and painted most movingly were, although not Puritans in the theological sense, men with some traits which would have appealed to the Puritans almost as much as they did to Parkman. They faced and conquered odds by their indomitable devotion to a great cause. Religious or not, they were heroes because they had and used the qualities of character by which the Puritan himself won his successes in the wilderness.

The influence of Puritan literary theories and habits

on the development of prose style and on later history
and biography was in part at least beneficent, but most
critics agree that with poetry the case is different. Some
of the Anglican religious poets of seventeenth-century
England won literary immortality; few of their Puritan
contemporaries, at home or in the colonies, did. The
inheritors of the American Puritan tradition, whatever
their merits, have rarely pleased the critics and readers
who delight in the lyrics of Donne, Herbert, and
Vaughan. They were handicapped by the "Puritan distrust of plastic richness as a snare for the eye," by the
Puritan's attitude toward the senses and the use of
sensuous material in religious art.[26] The situation was
not improved when pioneer Puritanism hardened down
into an organized and intolerant ecclesiastical and
creedal system. Verse became cooler and cooler and
farther from poetry. There were still versified expositions of pious precepts, rhymed paraphrases from the
Bible, verse narratives of God's providential acts, and
competent occasional stanzas on this or that New
England worthy or event, but there was little which
could not have been as well said in prose. The waning
of the original rebellious spirit of Puritanism weakened
the distrust of Anglican and Catholic forms of writing,
and New Englanders neatly, and often ingeniously,
aped the stylistic methods of the great English religious
poetry of the early seventeenth century, but they
still excluded much sensuous poetic material and their
verses were usually only pale exercises in superficial
imitation.

There is a kinship between the cool correctness of such poets as Bryant — Lowell spoke of his "ice-ola-tion" [27] — and the tradition of Puritanism turned conventional. Longfellow too, for all his expert craftsmanship, rarely lifts his poetic moralizing above the level of calm homage to a stereotyped formula. He was the heir not of pioneer but of later Puritanism, which relied too much on a formal code rather than on a deeply and personally realized belief. Emerson's occasional inability to fuse form and content in poetry, the curious flatness of much later New England verse, the dryness sometimes obvious in the work of Edwin Arlington Robinson, are all examples of the weaknesses of the Puritan poetic tradition. Now and then, notably in Emily Dickinson, something of the intensity of the pioneers flares up again, but in other poets the fruit of the tradition is too often correctness not vigor. Too often the flavor is bland and thin, and the effect is one of discipline carried to the point of emotional starvation. When James Russell Lowell said that he was

> striving Parnassus to climb
> With a whole bale of *isms* tied together with rhyme,[28]

he was making fun of his New England habit of using verse to prove a point or support a cause. That was the Puritan way, but the earliest colonists at their best wrote with an emotional force and conviction which, in spite of their "isms" and the handicaps of their theory, gave off poetic sparks. Lowell's New England was painfully inclined toward the prosaic attitudes of the later diluted

Puritanism, which discouraged robustness of heart and mind.

The tangible data of literary history cast some light on the relation of Puritan writing to later American literature, but such data never tell the whole story. The real forces in the growth of any literature can never be measured completely by changes in conventions of style or theme or by the formal development of literary genres. The fertilizing tradition is a matter of spirit and idea; the fruitful heritage of the past comes from ways of thought and feeling, fundamental intellectual and emotional points of view, which have the power to stimulate new attempts to map the changing current of life. Such things are hard to categorize; their nature defies precise definition. Their influence comes in large part from the fact that they are living organisms, not static entities which can be exactly measured and weighed.

It is particularly difficult to be confident as to the elements in Puritanism which did most to influence, in the fundamental sense of that word, American literature and American religious thought since the seventeenth century, because Puritanism was itself a complex of many elements, and because the main stream divided into several channels as it pursued its course in America. There have been many attempts to chart those channels, and the relation of Puritanism not only to later literature and religious thought but also to the broadest aspects of social and economic life has been much discussed. The evidence is rarely conclusive enough to support dogmatic assertions, but there are bases for reasonable conjectures. Even guesses have value, since they bear upon a strain in American intellectual history the existence of which few historians would doubt even though its exact nature may be impossible to define.

Shrewd critics of Puritanism have never been at a loss to find in it qualities unfortunately suggestive of the least Christian aspects of the America which the New England colonists helped to found. Just as its literary influence, in poetry at least, may be held to have been bad, it is possible to maintain that its influence on other concerns of life has been as bad or worse. Has not the colonists' confidence in the rightness of their theology and in their position as champions of God against error fostered bitter intolerance? Has not the Puritan's emphasis on sin bred in some of his descendants, deprived of the more constructive elements of his faith, a crippling sense of guilt? Has not his intense concentration on the individual spiritual life, revealed in his diaries or autobiographies, led now and then to pathological morbidness or, more serious, to an individualism which amounts to selfishness and social irresponsibility? Cannot the misuse of such phrases as "free enterprise" to mask socially destructive greed be easily explained as the product of Puritan individualism? Cannot contemporary emphasis on material values be explained by an inherited taint of Puritanism which exalts thrift and worldly success as marks of godliness? Answer these questions in the affirmative and you have a ready-made indictment of the Puritan tradition — an indictment which American critics during the 1920's repeatedly pressed.

Except for such overenthusiastic critics, a bare affirmative answer will not do. That the colonists were intolerant, no one can question; that their magnification of peccadilloes into major sins was, by contemporary standards, absurd, no one will challenge. The Puritan's distrust of the senses seems today like a partial denial of life; the dangers of his introspectiveness and his individualism, unless controlled by some positive principle, are painfully plain. But original Puritanism did have a positive principle. Michael Wigglesworth was tormented by his sense of his own iniquity, but he made for himself a successful and useful career as a minister, teacher, and citizen. However unhealthy his soul-searchings may seem, he never relapsed into idle neuroticism, but worked steadfastly to prove himself worthy of God's love. John Bunyan said: "No sin against God can be little, because it is against the great God of heaven and earth; but if the sinner can find out a little God, it may be easy to find out little sins." [29] Wigglesworth and other Puritans would have agreed. Their God was a great God; the labors required of his servants were onerous. Any lapse from his laws, however trivial, could not seem trivial to men who passionately loved and feared him. The magnitude of their conception of God and of their role as his servants eclipsed everything else, and both their love and their fear were compelling motives for a constant and exciting struggle to do his will. They were individualists, but as long as they genuinely centered their lives on a "great God" and thought of New England as the country of his chosen people, they avoided the worst selfishness and the most dangerously anti-social qualities of individualism unrestrained. They were not saints, and some of them were hypocrites, but many had faith and courage enough to come nearer than most of their descendants to a truly Christian life. The harshness, bleakness, and sterility which are commonly thought of as Puritan, conquered only when the pristine ardor waned, the "great God" dwindled, and obedience to his law was no longer dictated by a deeply felt inner need.

In literature also, what is best in the tradition of Puritanism comes from its original spirit, not from the hollow conformity into which it declined. The Puritans' real gifts to later writers were not the specific contributions to the development of techniques and types of writing which have already been commented upon, but a few general religious and moral attitudes which have had significant implications for the artists. In the genuine Puritan tradition, character and morality are seen as permanent values achievable only by personal spiritual conquest, life is constantly spiritualized, and the humblest events and acts are related to a divine context. A writer who accepts such views is sure to reflect them not only in the content of his work but in his theory of style.

Samuel Sewall went to a picnic in 1697 and ate a great deal — among other things, "very good Rost Lamb, Turkey, Fowls, Aplepy." After the meal, the company sang Psalm 121, and then, he writes, "A Glass of spirits my Wife sent stood upon a Joint-Stool which, Simon W. jogging, it fell down and broke all to shivers: I said 'twas a lively Emblem of our Fragility and Mortality." [30] In Sewall's mind there was no incongruity in following a hearty picnic by a psalm, or in reflecting piously on spilled liquor as a symbol of moral truth. Many New Englanders and many other Americans since 1697 have tried to see idealistic values in good business, have tried to link life, even in its commonplace aspects, with religion. Others have been leaders in reform and pioneers for new causes because their spiritual impulses seemed to them normally to coincide with concrete accomplishment in this world. In literature this has led to a constant emphasizing of moral values by the writers most susceptible to Puritan ways of thought. The result has been sometimes clumsy didacticism, but some major American artists have found rich suggestions for method and theme in the Puritan linking of the ideal with the concretely actual.

In Puritan theology Hawthorne found a set of concepts indispensable as the framework for his allegorical or symbolic presentations of moral drama. That he accepted neither the creed of the Puritans nor their polity mattered not at all. Their emphasis on sin, their consciousness of the adventurous struggle involved in spiritual development, and their taste for expressing the ideal in images and symbols of earth gave him not only his most characteristic themes but suggestions as to the best means of expressing concern with the inner life.

Melville thought that Hawthorne's "great power of blackness" derived "its force from its appeals to that Calvinistic sense of Innate Depravity and Original Sin, from whose visitations, in some shape or other, no deeply thinking mind is always and wholly free." [31] The last clause shows that Melville himself had felt the "force" of one basic element in Puritan thinking. Both Hawthorne and Melville "saw the empirical truth behind the Calvinist symbols" and "recovered what Puritans professed but seldom practiced — the spirit of piety, humility and tragedy in face of the inscrutable ways of God." [32] Apart from the moot question of the extent to which the Puritans' professions were carried out in practice, it is plain that Melville in all his best work from *Mardi* to *Billy Budd* drew something from their thought. Both he and Hawthorne were influenced also by the "tendency of American idealism to see a spiritual significance in every natural fact," a tendency "far more broadly diffused than transcendentalism." [33] Of it F. O. Matthiessen says, "Loosely Platonic, it came specifically from the common background that lay behind Emerson and Hawthorne, from the Christian habit of mind that saw the hand of God in all manifestations of life, and which, in the intensity of the New England seventeenth century, had gone to the extreme." [34] The relation between this background and Melville's and Hawthorne's use of concrete symbols to express ideal reality is obvious.

Puritan individualism has also left an indelible mark. One of our "grand national types of personality"

196

has been "the adventurous colonist; the Protestant sectarian, determined to worship his own God even in the wilderness." [35] In him, as in other American types, there were good elements and bad, but his ideas have stimulated artists working in a world unlike his and in times when his theology was forgotten. His concentration on the life of the spirit as the core of character and his exaltation of the morally enlightened individual above all restraints certainly gave clues to Hawthorne and Melville, as well as to Thoreau and Emerson. All four echoed something closely akin to the Puritan's personal belief that the foundation of holiness was the personal search for truth, even when a royal government, a powerful established church, and the terrors of the wilderness seemed to bar the way.

Another aspect of Puritan individualism is reflected in the work of later writers. It is an easy step from the colonists' anxious self-analysis to Hawthorne's care "for the deeper psychology," which both Henry James and T. S. Eliot recognized.[36] James felt a charm "even in Hawthorne's slightest allegories . . . which redeemed their stiffness for him," because they gave "glimpses of a great field, of the whole deep mystery of man's soul and conscience. They are moral, and their interest is moral; they deal with something more than the mere accidents and conventionalities, the surface occurrences of life." [37] The Puritan had his allegories too, and their charm for him was the same as Hawthorne's for James — which suggests that one thread of influence from Puritanism stretches well beyond Hawthorne and

Emerson and Melville to James and perhaps even to Eliot.

Part of the continuing power of the Puritan's ideas comes from the fact that he was not only an idealist but a nonconformist. So, in essential parts of their thought, have been most of the best New England writers since their time. They, like him, have asserted as both a right and duty man's obligation to think and live by his moral convictions, even when they ran counter to accepted beliefs. There is much in them of the devout early colonist who was a rebel, but neither in love with rebellion for its own sake or reckless in iconoclasm. He believed that his theology and his whole intellectual scheme were soundly based on the best authority of the past, and he believed that he attacked or destroyed only things which stood in the way of what could rationally and logically be proved good. He was, he believed, not the creature of passion, but the servant of reason.

Nonconformity of this sort, coupled with Puritan idealism, accounts for some of the noblest aspects of later American thought and writing. Emerson was by no means a whole-hearted admirer of the Puritans and recognized that before his time they had "declined into ritualists," but he believed their virtues were still needed. For him the pioneer New Englanders were "great, grim, earnest men," who had "solemnized the heyday of their strength by the planting and liberating of America." [38] "This town of Boston has a history," he said.

It is not an accident, not a windmill, or a railroad station, or crossroads tavern, or an army-barracks grown up by time and luck to a place of wealth; but a seat of humanity, of men of principle, obeying a sentiment and marching loyally whither that should lead them . . . I do not speak with any fondness, but the language of coldest history, when I say that Boston commands attention as the town which was appointed in the destiny of nations to lead the civilization of North America.[39]

Emerson is thinking of the moral tradition of Boston, as the Puritans did, and his very imagery suggests theirs. Just as they loved to symbolize themselves as an army of righteousness, so he pictures his men of principle as "marching loyally." And just as the Puritans reverenced history and believed that the success of their colonial venture was proof that they were carrying out God's will, so Emerson is sure that Boston was by destiny appointed to lead civilization on this continent. The terms are shifted from the theological, but the spirit remains the same.

Emerson also touches specifically on the Puritan tradition of idealism and of nonconformity. "These Englishmen," he says of the pioneer settlers, "with the Middle Ages still obscuring their reason, were filled with Christian thought. They had a culture of their own . . . They were precisely the idealists of England; the most religious in a religious era." [40] He drives his point home with an image of just the sort which the Puritans themselves delighted in. He writes: "An old lady who remembered these pious people said of them that 'they had to hold on hard to the huckle-

berry bushes to hinder themselves from being translated.'" [41] "As an antidote to the spirit of commerce
and of economy," Emerson goes on, "the religious
spirit — always enlarging, firing man, prompting the
pursuit of the vast, the beautiful, the unattainable —
was especially necessary to the culture of New England." [42] As for nonconformity,

> Boston never wanted a good principle of rebellion in it, from
> the planting until now; there is always a minority unconvinced
> . . . some protester against the cruelty of the magistrates to the
> Quakers . . . some defender of the slave against the politician
> and the merchant; some champion of first principles of humanity
> against the rich and luxurious . . . some pleader for peace;
> some noble protestant, who will not stoop to infamy when all
> are gone mad, but will stand for liberty and justice, if alone,
> until all come back to him. [43]

Of course, Emerson admits that New England's history
contains many dark chapters of cruelty and injustice,
but he insists that it should be judged by its best, which,
as he defines it, bears the unmistakable marks of its
Puritan heritage. Boston "is very willing to be out-
numbered and outgrown" by other cities, "full of its
blood and name and traditions," if those cities will
"carry forward its life of civil and religious freedom,
of education, of social order, and of loyalty to law . . .
It owes its existence and its power to principles not of
yesterday, and the deeper principle will always pre-
vail." [44]

Today the Puritans' dream of what the New England colonies might become is unrealized, and the

Boston which Emerson praised has ceased to be — if, indeed, it ever existed. The United States bears little resemblance to anything that the colonists or Emerson thought a great nation should be. Much good Puritan seed fell on ground so barren that the fruit was dwarfed and sour. Too often only the narrowness and intolerance of Puritanism survived; too often its more generous spirit was lost. In practice, when it commanded the hearts and minds of the colonists, it "was the most strenuous of creeds" and "the greatest of the Puritans, far from yielding fatalistically to some superior will, asserted their own wills at every turn with the resoluteness and vehemence of men for whom freedom is an unchallenged reality." [45] Today little of their moral robustness persists, and it is hard to find any faith, or even any intellectual system, which is as stimulating and as productive of useful action as was the faith and system of the Puritans when they laid the foundations of their Bible commonwealth.

This does not mean that the relation of Puritan theology to Puritan literature, and their influence, good and bad, are without significance today. The Puritans in their heyday used their faith as an incentive to action, some of the fruits of which their successors still enjoy, and their faith was nourished by the written and spoken word. Their writings satisfied and stimulated their audience, helped men and women to find strength in a conception of God-centered universe, and encouraged them to turn their beliefs into action. They built a new state not simply with axes and spades but with books, the best pages of which deserve immortality because they give fitting expression to essential values and profoundly felt emotions. That this country is no longer Puritan is not the point, nor does it matter that the Puritan creed and polity in New England eventually gave way to other beliefs and ways of worship. The religious literature of the colonies is still important if for no other reason than that it sheds light on some aspects of the relation between religion and art, and on some problems which are as acute for the contemporary religious artist as they were for the seventeenth-century writers in Massachusetts.

They did their work well. Much, perhaps most, of what they wrote has lost its power now, but little of it failed of its purpose when it was fresh from the press. Today, on the other hand, it is hard to find any considerable body of genuinely religious literature capable of serving its times as well as the colonists' books served theirs, or likely to enjoy the continuing influence which they have had. If this is true it is a fact to be seriously weighed, since it seems incontestable that vigor of religious thought and feeling must always depend in part upon the means by which thought and feeling can be communicated — in other words, upon religious literature, spoken or written. Dogmatism as to the lessons to be learned from the way in which the Puritan wrote in the service of his faith would be dangerous; but it is not unreasonable to seek in his success suggestions as to the reasons for our failures.

Chancellor Hutchins of the University of Chicago

is said to have made a remark some years ago to the effect that "the reason America no longer wants the college, is because the college has given America what it wants." The truth within the paradox is one with which many educators would heartily agree. Education depends upon leadership, upon the stimulation of students to aspire to something higher and better than they would otherwise seek. It should be a training of minds to use their full powers and a source of material to tax those powers. If education instead caters only to what men and women think they want and is content to supply only what they find easy or are prepared to accept as by their standards practically useful, it inevitably loses its real value. The value once lost, students turn away disgusted with the discovery that they have been given nothing more than they already had.

There is a reasonable analogy between this and some of the religious problems of today. If religion involves no hard thought, no struggle, no sacrifice, no stimulus to all of the human faculties, it may well miss its major opportunity. If sermons and books merely appease their audiences and demand no more intellectually or emotionally than a football game, a crossword puzzle, or a cheap novel, they are likely to furnish no more than a drowsy hour or two of smug self-satisfaction for the man who supposes them to be "good" by virtue of their theme. They will usually give even less stimulation to thought than the humdrum routine of business and less pleasure than the anesthetic effects of aimless recreation. Such stimulation and pleasure were too weak for the

Puritan. He studied diligently and trained himself in logic and rhetoric in order to learn the truth and to be able to communicate it intelligibly, but he did not cheat himself and his audience by watering down his thought or his style to the point of tastelessness. He spared his readers and hearers many of the stubborn technicalities that had interest only for scholars, but he did not mitigate in the slightest the full and terrifying import of his conception of God, of Heaven, of Hell, of fallen man, and of the arduousness of the life of faith. The popular appeal he made was in terms of language and imagery. He chose the words that were most evocative for the people he addressed, but he used them to elevate tastes, to increase understanding, and to prepare the hearts and minds of his hearers and readers to receive, if it were vouchsafed, the ultimate gift of faith. He knew that there were love, joy, and release from fear to be found in religion, but believed that they could not be had for the asking, or attained by thoughtless passivity. He was sure that to stoop to flashy tricks of style would be to gain nothing but a minute's applause; his interest was in the slow process by which man might be led to matured individual conviction and a genuine realization of the mystery of holiness. It is possible, without in the least endorsing the grimmer aspects of his creed and without binding ourselves by the artistic limitations within which he worked, profitably to take a leaf from his book and to strive for a religious literature, spoken and written, designed not merely to please momentarily but to challenge men and women to try their full capacities in the service of religion or the search for it. Emerson had no use for the strict Puritan theology, but he understood the role of the religious artist and declared that when literature is "in the right hands," it "is not resorted to as consolation, but as decalogue." [46]

It is possible that contemporary religious life has suffered from a tendency of religious writers toward tender-mindedness rather than tough-mindedness. Too many of them have let sentimentality or loosely defined doctrine replace soundly phrased emotion and sturdily reasoned teaching. Robert Louis Stevenson said, "It is not strange if we are tempted to despair of good — our religions and moralities have been trimmed to flatter us, till they are all emasculate and sentimentalised, and only please and weaken. Truth is of a rougher strain. In the harsh face of life faith can read a bracing gospel." [47] The great days of Puritanism were the days when men of passionate conviction worked hard and long not to dilute their teaching so that anyone might sit placidly through a sermon or unthinkingly read a religious book, but to bring the simplest auditor up to the point where he could rejoice in using his full powers to realize the meaning of life according to divine law.

The Puritans' theology was shaped to the nature of existence, as they saw it. It accounted for the evil they found in men and in society; it gave them special hope because their ultimate salvation, predestined by God, depended wholly on God's choice and in no way on their worldly status or the social barriers erected against them as middle-class folk. There might be no democracy on this earth, but they were originally equal in the sight of God, and such distinctions as had been drawn between them by divine predestination had been drawn without reference to their worldly rank, wealth, or power. They were, except for God's grace, helpless and vile, but each of them might hope that God had selected him to be redeemed. This hope was a surer comfort than any confidence they can have had that they could in this world achieve equality with those who in economic and social terms claimed superiority to them.

This suggests a query as to whether contemporary religion can boast of any similarly consistent relation to the actual facts of current life, and as to whether it has any developed myth or set of symbols that can typify imaginatively and emotionally in dramatic terms its principles and standards. Are there religious writers today who can express for our times as vividly as Puritan poets, biographers, and historians did for theirs, the actual meaning of Christian faith and Christian action? Has religious literature today mastered language and imagery as close to the actual everyday needs and aspirations of men and women as the language and imagery of the Puritans? Is our religious thinking consistent and firm enough to support a genuinely effective myth? If not, we are not likely to match the Puritan in earnestness or to give to our religion the vitality he gave to his.

Booksellers and publishers still find a great demand

for "religious books," but it is very hard to find any workable definition of what such a book is. There are novels, historical in material and largely sentimental in tone; there are volumes which, if they were not written by clerics, would almost certainly be classified under psychology or sociology rather than religion or theology. The symptoms unhappily suggest that, instead of knowing as the Puritan did what he meant by the religious life, and instead of centering it on a consistent and reasoned theology, many contemporary writers confuse religion with other things. It has been said that the minister today is not in the old sense a minister at all, but a practicing sociologist or psychiatrist. If this is true, sociological treatises or psychiatric manuals written by amateurs may be the modern substitutes for Puritan poems, history, biography, or sermons. There are unpleasant signs that the minister today sometimes sacrifices soundness of doctrine to popular appeal and still finds it hard to make his congregation think of religion as anything but an amiable survival of the past to be talked about lazily on an occasional idle Sunday. If the signs are to be trusted, it is easy to explain why mawkish and sensational novels which deal with the past and are read as an escape from the pressing concerns of the present continue to climb into the best-sellers' list. If religion has become simply a matter of sentimental revery, looking backward, or if its rationalism has forced it to yield its position to some science or branch of medicine, it does not need religious literature of the kind that the seventeenth century loved.

If, on the other hand, the phenomenon of religious experience is still real for some men; if there is a place for a faith transcending what unaided reason, logic, or science can supply; if there is still value in the prayer and worship which proceed from deep inward emotion, then scientific manuals, polite moral essays, and popular novels will not suffice. There will be need for more intellectually incisive and more emotionally effective expression of contemporary religious life; there will be need for some myth in which to symbolize and concretize its values. Myths are given life by artists; a way of life or of thought, a doctrine or an ideal that is to become part of the shaping consciousness of a society, must have artists to give it imaginative vitality and form. If it is certain that contemporary religious life is healthy in all respects, there is nothing to be learned from the Puritan colonists; but if it seems, as the rebellious Puritan's life in Europe seemed to him, in need of new strength, it is reasonable to ask whether present-day Americans might not profit, as he did, by setting not only the rationalist and the logician but the artist to work.

How he should work, and with what material, are questions for him and for theologians to solve. He will have little to learn from the technical devices and forms used by the Puritans, and he will need to avoid their mistakes. He must not open himself to Henry Adams's charge against Emerson: "In obtaining extreme sublimation or tenuity of intelligence, I infer that sensuousness must be omitted";[48] but he may learn much from the Puritans' insistence that the expression must be integrally related to the essentials of the theology. The theologians, for their part, may dismiss all the superficial tenets of Puritanism, but they must somehow construct for our times a reading of Christian truth which is as relevant to our society as the Puritan's was for his.

Both theologian and artist might well ponder Samuel Sewall's:

As long as *Plum Island* shall faithfully keep the commanded Post: Notwithstanding all the hectoring Words, and hard Blows of the proud and boisterous Ocean; As long as any Salmon, or Sturgeon shall swim in the streams of *Merrimack*; or any Perch, or Pickeril, in *Crane-Pond*; As long as the Sea-Fowl shall know the Time of their coming, and not neglect seasonably to visit the Places of their Acquaintance; As long as any Cattel shall be fed with the Grass growing in the Medows, which do humbly bow down themselves before *Turkie-Hill*; As long as any Sheep shall walk upon *Old Town Hills*, and shall from thence pleasantly look down upon the River *Parker*, and the fruitfull *Marishes* lying beneath; As long as any free and harmless Doves shall find a White Oak, or other Tree within the Township, to perch, or feed, or build a careless Nest upon; and shall voluntarily present themselves to perform the office of Gleaners after Barley-Harvest; As long as Nature shall not grow Old and dote; but shall constantly remember to give the rows of Indian Corn their education, by Pairs: So long shall Christians be born there; and being first made meet, shall from thence be Translated, to be made partakers of the Inheritance of the Saints in Light.[49]

Plum Island is much changed since Sewall's day, but it still withstands the proud ocean's hectoring violence; birds still nest in white oaks; the Parker River still makes its way through the salt marshes to the sea. Theology has much changed too, but we may hope, with Sewall, that Christians are still being born, and "being first made meet," are preparing themselves to be "partakers of the Inheritance of the Saints." If so, true religious life will be well served indeed if artists of today prove as skillful as Sewall, two hundred and fifty years ago, in clothing a religious aspiration in images as imaginatively moving as Sewall's invocation of hill and sea and stream. His love for his own countryside and for the God he served enabled him to write, in one paragraph at least, memorable prose. Nor will artists fail today if matured and truly religious principles and the heartfelt aspiration of a society call upon them once more to dedicate their best talents to the service of a noble faith.

NOTES

ACKNOWLEDGMENTS

FOR THE USE OF QUOTATIONS

Basil Blackwell: Ben Jonson, *Poems*, ed. B. H. Newdigate. The Bassett Estate: *The Middle Group of American Historians*, by John S. Bassett. Bruce Publishing Company: *Christian Life and Worship*, by Gerald Ellard. Cassell and Company: *Puritanism and Art: An Inquiry into a Popular Fallacy*, by Joseph Crouch. Charles Scribner's Sons: "Pulvis et Umbra," in R. L. Stevenson, *Works* (Thistle ed.). Clarendon Press, Oxford: *English Literature in the Earlier Seventeenth Century*, by Douglas Bush; *Oxford Book of Christian Verse*, ed. Lord David Cecil; Richard Crashaw, *The Poems, English, Latin, and Greek*, ed. L. C. Martin; *The Poems of John Donne*, ed. H. J. C. Grierson; *Essays, Historical & Literary*, by Sir Charles Firth; George Herbert, *Works*, ed. F. E. Hutchinson; *The Poems and Letters of Andrew Marvell*, ed. H. M. Margoliouth; *Critical Essays of the Seventeenth Century*, ed. J. E. Spingarn; *Elizabethan and Jacobean*, by F. P. Wilson. Columbia University Press: *The Rise of Puritanism*, by William Haller. Encyclopædia Britannica: "History," by J. T. Shotwell. Ernest Benn, Ltd.: *Protestantism*, by W. R. Inge. Faber and Faber Limited: *The High Church Tradition, a Study in the Liturgical Thought of the Seventeenth Century*, by G. W. O. Addleshaw. Harcourt, Brace and Company, Inc.: *The Diary of Samuel Pepys*, ed. H. B. Wheatley; *Some Religious Elements in English Literature*, by Rose Macaulay. Houghton Mifflin Company: *A Memoir of Ralph Waldo Emerson*, by J. E. Cabot; *Henry Adams and His Friends*, ed. H. D. Cater; *The Complete Works of Ralph Waldo Emerson*, ed. E. W. Emerson; *Journals of Ralph Waldo Emerson*, ed. E. W. Emerson and W. E. Forbes; *The Writings of James Russell Lowell* (Riverside ed.); *The Writings of Henry David Thoreau* (Walden ed.). Jonathan Cape, Limited: *The Reverend Richard Baxter; Under the Cross (1662–1691)*, by F. J. Powicke. Little, Brown & Company: *Hawthorne*, by Newton Arvin. Louisiana State University Press: *Richard Crashaw, a Study in Baroque Sensibility*, by Austin Warren. Macmillan Company: *History of Religion in the United States*, by H. K. Rowe (Copyright, 1924 by The Macmillan Company); *The Heart of the Yale Lectures*, by Batsell B. Baxter (Copyright, 1947 by The Macmillan Company); *The Miltonic Setting Past & Present*, by E. M. W. Tillyard (Cambridge University Press); *The New England Mind: The Seventeenth Century*, by Perry Miller (Copyright, 1929, by The Macmillan Company). New England Quarterly: "Some Edward Taylor Gleanings," by Thomas H. Johnson. Oxford University Press: *American Renaissance*, by F. O. Matthiessen (Copyright 1941 by Oxford University Press, Inc.). Princeton University Press: *The Poetical Works of Edward Taylor*, ed. Thomas H. Johnson. Sheed and Ward: *The English Way, Studies in English Sanctity from St. Bede to Newman*, ed. Maisie Ward. University of Wisconsin Press: *English Devotional Literature (Prose), 1600–1640*, by Helen C. White. William and Mary Quarterly: "Biographical Technique in Cotton Mather's *Magnalia*," by R. E. Watters.

I. THE BACKGROUND:
THE GOLDEN AGE OF ENGLISH RELIGIOUS LITERATURE

1. Rose Macaulay, *Some Religious Elements in English Literature* (New York, 1931), p. 84.

2. Francis Bacon, *Advancement of Learning* in *The Works of Francis Bacon*, edited by J. Spedding, R. L. Ellis, and D. D. Heath (Boston, 1861), VI, 392.

3. Helen C. White, *English Devotional Literature (Prose), 1600–1640* (Madison, 1931), p. 10.

4. White, p. 236.

5. H. O. Taylor, *The Mediaeval Mind* (New York, 1919), II, 427.

6. These quotations were included, as quotations, in an address by John Livingston Lowes at a symposium on "Religion and the Arts" on November 9, 1926. A shorthand version of the address was printed in the *Harvard Alumni Bulletin*, XXIX, 409–413 (January 13, 1927).

7. *Harvard Alumni Bulletin*, XXIX, 410.

8. Austin Warren, *Richard Crashaw, A Study in Baroque Sensibility* (University, La., 1939), p. 66.

9. *Ibid.*

10. Joseph Crouch, *Puritanism and Art. An Inquiry into a Popular Fallacy* (London, 1910), p. 25.

11. Richard Crashaw, *The Poems, English, Latin, and Greek*, edited by L. C. Martin (Oxford, 1927), p. 99.

12. "The Flaming Heart," in *Poems*, pp. 326–327.

13. E. I. Watkin, "Richard Crashaw," in *The English Way, Studies in English Sanctity from St. Bede to Newman*, edited by Maisie Ward (London, 1933), pp. 279–282.

14. Gerald Ellard, *Christian Life and Worship* (revised and enlarged ed.; Milwaukee, 1940), pp. 68, 71.

15. Ellard, p. 370.

16. Ellard, pp. 68, 234.

17. Ellard, p. 77.

18. Ellard, p. 219.

19. Warren, *Crashaw*, p. 67.

20. Warren, p. 75.

21. Warren, p. 76.

22. Warren, p. 66.

23. Unsigned review in the *Times* (London) *Literary Supplement* for July 13, 1940.

24. *The Oxford Book of Christian Verse,* edited by Lord David Cecil (Oxford, 1940), pp. xii–xiii.

25. Unsigned review cited in note 23 above.

26. Letter of Emerson to his wife, January 8, 1843, quoted in James E. Cabot, *A Memoir of Ralph Waldo Emerson* (Boston, 1887), II, 472.

27. G. W. O. Addleshaw, *The High Church Tradition, A Study in the Liturgical Thought of the Seventeenth Century* (London, 1941), p. 16.

28. White, *English Devotional Literature,* pp. 238–239.

29. "An Apologie for the Precedent Hymne," in *Poems,* p. 137.

30. Jean F. Senault, *The Use of Passions* (London, 1649), pp. 102–103, quoted in Perry Miller, *The New England Mind. The Seventeenth Century* (New York, 1939), p. 257.

31. "The Accusation of the Inward Man," in *The Poetical Works of Edward Taylor,* edited by Thomas H. Johnson (New York, 1939), p. 55.

32. George Herbert, "The H. Communion," in *Works,* edited by F. E. Hutchinson (Oxford, 1941), p. 52.

33. A. Marvell, "A Dialogue Between the Resolved Soul, and Created Pleasure," in *The Poems and Letters of Andrew Marvell,* edited by H. M. Margoliouth (Oxford, 1927), I, 10–12.

34. W. R. Inge, *Protestantism* (Garden City, 1928), p. 75.

35. *Works,* p. 246.

36. *Works,* p. 246.

37. *Works,* pp. 109–110.

38. *Works,* p. 131.

39. *The Poems of John Donne,* edited by H. J. C. Grierson (Oxford, 1912), I, 345, 347.

40. *Works,* p. 206.

41. *Works,* p. 115.

42. Sermon preached at Whitehall, February 12, 1618, quoted in Evelyn M. Simpson, *A Study of the Prose Works of John Donne* (Oxford, 1924), p. 237.

43. *Works,* pp. 67–68.

II. THE PURITAN LITERARY ATTITUDE

1. Samuel Whiting's life of John Cotton, printed in Alexander Young, *Chronicles of the First Planters of Massachusetts Bay* (Boston, 1846), pp. 421–422.

2. Cotton Mather, *Magnalia Christi Americana*, book III, part I, chapter 1, paragraph 4. I have quoted the text of the 1855 Hartford edition.

3. Thomas Hooker, *The Soules Preparation for Christ* (London, 1632), p. 66.

4. Increase Mather, *The Life and Death of . . . Mr. Richard Mather*, reprinted in *Collections of the Dorchester Antiquarian and Historical Society*, no. 3 (Boston, 1850), p. 85.

5. Ebenezer Turell, *Ministers should carefully avoid giving Offense in any Thing* (Boston, 1740), p. 15.

6. Perry Miller and Thomas H. Johnson, *The Puritans* (New York, 1938), p. 289.

7. *The Works of John Donne*, edited by Henry Alford (London, 1839), IV, 236.

8. *Works*, I, 71–72.

9. Richard Baxter, *Gildas Salvianus; The First Part: i.e., The Reformed Pastor* (London, 1656), p. 123; Valentine Marshall, "To the Reader," in Richard Capel, *Remains* (London, 1658).

10. "The Crosse," in *Poems*, I, 332.

11. R. Cudworth, *A Sermon Preached Before the Honourable House of Commons . . .* March 31, 1647 (Cambridge, 1647), pp. 25, 5.

12. Sir Thomas Browne, *Religio Medici*, part I, section 11.

13. *Works of . . . Richard Hooker* (Oxford, 1807), I, 200.

14. Miller, *New England Mind*, p. 10.

15. John Preston, *Life Eternall, Or, A Treatise of the Knowledge of the Divine Essence* (London, 1631), part I, p. 101.

16. H. C. Beeching, *Religio Laici* (London, 1902), p. 79.

17. Thomas Blount, *Glossographia* (London, 1656), s.v. "Enthusiasts."

18. White, *English Devotional Literature*, pp. 231–232, 233.

19. John Downame, *Christian Warfare* (London, 1609), pp. 339, 341, 342.

20. Downame, p. 339.

21. Downame, pp. 340–341.
22. I Corinthians 14:9.
23. Letter to Henry Dodwell, quoted in Frederick J. Powicke, *The Reverend Richard Baxter; Under the Cross (1662–1691)* (London, 1927), p. 224.
24. Manuscript, quoted by Powicke, p. 276.
25. I. Mather, *Life and Death*, p. 85.
26. Crouch, *Puritanism and Art*, p. 199.
27. Downame, *Christian Warfare*, p. 342.
28. Richard Baxter, *A Saint or a Brute* (London, 1662), prefatory letter "To my dearly beloved Friends."
29. William Perkins, "The Art of Prophecying," in *Workes* (London, 1612–1613), II, 670.
30. John Geree, *The Character of an Old English-Puritan* (London, 1659), p. 2.
31. *The Complete Works of Richard Sibbes*, edited by Alexander B. Grosart (Edinburgh, 1862–1864), I, ci.
32. William Ames, "Briefe Premonition" prefixed to "The Marrow of Sacred Divinity," in *Workes* (London, 1642).
33. Richard Baxter, *Poetical Fragments* (London, 1821), pp. ii, iii.
34. *Poetical Fragments*, p. v.
35. *Poetical Fragments*, p. 29.
36. *Poetical Fragments*, pp. i, ii.
37. *Poetical Fragments*, p. ii.
38. Richard Baxter, *The Saints Everlasting Rest* (7th ed.; London, 1658), pp. 749–751 (part IV, chap. xi, section 1).
39. *Ibid.*
40. *Ibid.*
41. *Saints Everlasting Rest*, pp. 751–753 (part IV, chap. xi, section 2).
42. Samuel Clarke, *The Lives of Thirty-Two English Divines* (3d ed.; London, 1677), p. 177.
43. *Reliquiae Baxterianae*, edited by Matthew Sylvester (London, 1696), lib. I, part 1, p. 137.
44. William Haller, *The Rise of Puritanism* (New York, 1938), p. 134.
45. Richard Bernard, *The Faithful Shepheard* (London, 1607), p. 65.

46. Thomas Shepard, "Of Ineffectual Hearing," in *Subjection to Christ* (London, 1654), p. 167.

47. William Hubbard, *The Happiness of a People* (Boston, 1676), p. 29.

48. John Bunyan, *The Pilgrim's Progress* (London, 1678). "The Author's Apology for his Book."

49. Sermon, "Culpable Ignorance," in Thomas Hooker, *The Saints Dignitie and Dutie* (London, 1651), p. 209.

50. Sermon, "The Preparing of the Heart," in Thomas Hooker, *The Soules Implantation* (London, 1637), p. 50.

51. John Cotton, *Christ The Fountaine of Life* (London, 1651), pp. 71–72.

52. Thomas Hooker, *The Application of Redemption* (2d ed.; London, 1659), pp. 210–211, 213–214.

53. Thomas Shepard, *The Sincere Convert* (London, 1655), p. 113.

54. *Sincere Convert*, pp. 14–15.

55. Cf. Miller, *New England Mind*, p. 327, and *passim*, and Miller and Johnson, *Puritans*, especially pp. 32–41 and 73–74. Even without Ramus, Puritan writing would probably have been essentially the same, since what his rules required was demanded also by the Puritans' theological tenets, the character of their audience, and other factors pointed out in this chapter. Mr. F. P. Wilson in a note in his *Elizabethan and Jacobean* (Oxford, 1945), p. 137, after praising Miller's work, comments: "But while Calvinists were glad to defend their methods by the doctrine of Ramus, their attachment to dialectics rather than rhetoric is too deep-rooted to be attributed to the influence of one man."

56. I. Mather, *Life and Death*, p. 85.

III. PURITAN HISTORIANS: "THE LORD'S REMEMBRANCERS"

1. For discussions of the Puritan sermon see, for example, Miller, *New England Mind*, especially chap. xii; Miller and Johnson, *Puritans*, especially pp. 64–74; W. Fraser Mitchell, *English Pulpit Oratory from Andrewes to Tillotson* (London, 1932), especially chaps. vii and x; Haller, *Rise of Puritanism*, especially chap. iv;

Caroline F. Richardson, *English Preachers and Preaching* (New York, 1928), *passim*; and Babette M. Levy, *Preaching in the First Half Century of New England History* (Hartford, 1945).

2. Ben Jonson, *Poems*, edited by B. H. Newdigate (Oxford, 1936), p. 125.

3. H. O. Taylor, *Thought and Expression in the Sixteenth Century* (New York, 1920), I, 356; Sir Thomas North, "To The Reader," in *The Lives of the Noble Grecians and Romanes . . . by Plutarke* (London, 1895–96), I, 7.

4. Sir Walter Raleigh, "Preface" in *The History of the World* (11th ed.; London, 1736), I, iii.

5. *Elizabethan Critical Essays*, edited by G. Gregory Smith (Oxford, 1904), I, 162ff., II, 40ff.

6. Cotton Mather, *Magnalia Christi Americana* (London, 1702), general introduction (vol. I, p. 29 in the Hartford, 1855, edition).

7. *The Histories of Polybius*, translated by Evelyn S. Shuckburgh (London, 1889), I, 1.

8. *Magnalia*, general introduction (vol. I, pp. 28–29 in the Hartford, 1855, edition).

9. Francis Bacon, *Advancement of Learning*, in *Works*, VI, 188–189.

10. Douglas Bush, *English Literature in the Earlier Seventeenth Century* (Oxford, 1945), p. 209.

11. Bush, p. 210.

12. James T. Shotwell, "History," in *Encyclopaedia Britannica* (Chicago, 1945). This article gives a valuable summary of historiography before the Puritan period. See also Shotwell's *The History of History* (New York, 1939), a revision of his *An Introduction to the History of History*; James W. Thompson, *History of Historical Writing* (New York, 1942); and especially Edward Fueter, *Geschichte der Neuren Historiographie* (3d ed.; Munich, 1936). Fueter's opinion of the influence of the Reformation writers on "scientific" history differs somewhat from that quoted from Shotwell; cf. Fueter, pp. 246–47.

13. In the second edition, Basel, 1624, some passages were altered to adapt them to the Calvinistic position. Fueter, pp. 249–250.

14. Shotwell, "History."

15. See Fueter, p. 253.

16. Fueter, p. 257.

17. For Foxe and his book, see Fueter, pp. 253–257.

18. *The Records of the Virginia Company of London,* edited by Susan M. Kingsbury (Washington, 1906–1935), I, 451–452.

19. Sir Charles Firth, "Sir Walter Raleigh's 'History of the World,'" in *Essays, Historical & Literary* (Oxford, 1938), pp. 44–45.

20. Edmund Bolton, "Hypercritica," in *Critical Essays of the Seventeenth Century,* edited by J. E. Spingarn (Oxford, 1908–1909), I, 84.

21. Firth, *Essays,* p. 44.

22. Raleigh, "Preface," I, iii, iv.

23. See Miller and Johnson, *Puritans,* chapter i, "History," especially p. 83.

24. William Bradford, *History of Plymouth Plantation,* edited by Worthington C. Ford (Boston, 1912), chapter i.

25. Bradford, I, 1.

26. Bradford, I, 120.

27. Bradford, I, 1.

28. Bradford, I, 96.

29. Bradford, I, 391.

30. Bradford, I, 386.

31. Bradford, I, 376–377; II, 76; I, 384.

32. Bradford, I, 363–364.

33. Bradford, I, 367.

34. Bradford, I, 380.

35. Bradford, I, 155–156.

36. Bradford, I, 156–158.

37. Bradford, I, 124.

38. *Johnson's Wonder-Working Providence,* edited by J. Franklin Jameson (New York, 1910), p. 22.

39. Johnson, p. 23.

40. Johnson, pp. 271–272.

41. Johnson, p. 151.

42. Miller, *New England Mind,* p. 106.

43. Nathaniel Morton, *New Englands Memoriall,* edited by Howard J. Hall (New York, 1937), p. iii.

44. Urian Oakes, *New England Pleaded With* (Cambridge, 1673), p. 23.

45. *Records of the Governor and Company of the Massachusetts Bay*, edited by N. B. Shurtleff (Boston, 1853–54), V, 378.

46. Bradford, *History of Plymouth*, I, 287, 436; Morton, *New Englands Memoriall*, pp. 41, 62.

47. Morton, *New Englands Memoriall*, "Epistle Dedicatory."

48. Morton, *New Englands Memoriall*, "To the Christian Reader."

49. Morton, p. 1.

50. Morton, *New Englands Memoriall*, "To the Christian Reader."

51. I. Mather, "A Brief History of the War with the Indians," in *The History of King Philip's War*, edited by Samuel G. Drake (Boston, 1862), p. 206.

52. *History of King Philip's War*, pp. 36–37.

IV. THE "PERSONAL LITERATURE" OF
THE PURITANS

1. E. M. W. Tillyard, *The Miltonic Setting Past & Present* (Cambridge, 1938), p. 78.

2. Haller, *Rise of Puritanism*, p. 96.

3. *The Diary of Samuel Pepys*, edited by H. B. Wheatley (London, 1924), VIII, 313, entry for May 31, 1699.

4. White, *English Devotional Literature*, pp. 224–225.

5. This has not been completely published, but Professor E. S. Morgan of Brown University has made an accurate transcription of it, deciphering the many shorthand passages.

6. Haller, *Rise of Puritanism*, pp. 38–39.

7. The diary is printed in *Massachusetts Historical Society Collections*, series 5, vols. V–VII (Boston, 1878–1882). The quoted passage is from V, 11.

8. Sewall, V, 38–39.

9. Sewall, V, 46, 47.

10. Sewall, V, 47.

11. The diary is printed in *Massachusetts Historical Society Collections*, series 7, vols. VII and VIII (Boston, 1911–1912). The quotations are from VII, 437–438.

12. The best edition of the autobiography is that printed in *Publications of the Colonial Society of Massachusetts*, XXVII, (Boston, 1932), 345–400. The quotation is from p. 352.

13. Shepard, p. 356.

14. Shepard, pp. 358–360.

15. Shepard, p. 361.

16. Shepard, p. 362.

17. Shepard, pp. 375, 393.

18. Shepard, pp. 391, 392.

19. Shepard, pp. 358, 360.

20. Shepard, p. 363.

21. Quoted in Haller, *Rise of Puritanism*, p. 95, from Thomas Goodwin, Jr., "Life," in Thomas Goodwin, *Works* (London, 1681–1704), vol. V.

22. John Norton, *Abel being Dead yet speaketh* (London, 1658), p. 3.

23. Norton, p. 4.

24. Norton, p. 5.

25. Norton, p. 15.

26. Norton, p. 19.

27. Norton, p. 34.

28. Norton, p. 45.

29. *Ibid.*

30. Norton, p. 23.

31. Norton, p. 24.

32. Norton, p. 26.

33. Norton, p. 31.

34. Norton, p. 34.

35. Norton, p. 35.

36. I. Mather, *Life and Death*, p. 57.

37. R. E. Watters in his "Biographical Technique in Cotton Mather's *Magnalia*" in *The William and Mary Quarterly* (April 1945), p. 154n., estimates that there are in the *Magnalia* about thirty-five lives of 500 to 2000 words, about twenty of 2000 to 4000, and 20 others of more than 4000, in addition to a "great number" of sketches of less than 500 words.

38. Samuel Clarke (1599–1683) was an assiduous writer of lives of the pious; Edmund Calamy (1671–1732) wrote *An Account of the Ejected Ministers . . .* (London, 1702), which is a

collection of short lives of the seventeenth-century divines excluded from the Church of England as nonconformists.

39. Izaak Walton, *The Life of Dr. Robert Sanderson* (London, 1678). The quotation is from the text as given in Geoffrey Keynes's edition of Walton's *Angler* and *Lives* (London, 1929), p. 500.

40. Baxter's book was printed in London in 1681. It was reprinted in John T. Wilkinson, *Richard Baxter and Margaret Charlton* (London, 1948); the best edition of Lucy Hutchinson's "Memoirs" of her husband is that by C. H. Firth (London, 1885).

41. Samuel Whiting's contemporary life of John Cotton was printed by Thomas Hutchinson in *A Collection of Original Papers Relative to the History of the Colony of Massachusetts Bay* (Boston, 1769) and reprinted in Young, *Chronicles of the First Planters of . . . Massachusetts Bay*; Turell, *The Life and Character of the Reverend Benjamin Colman* was published in Boston in 1749; his *Memoirs of the Life and Death of the Pious and Ingenious Mrs. Jane Turell* in Boston in 1735. His theme was "still the pilgrimage of man and woman from earth to heaven" but he sounds a new note in that his wife is called "not only 'pious' but 'ingenious' . . . She had 'digested' English poetry and was versed in 'polite pieces in prose'" and charmed Turell by her "taste" as well as her piety. "When such criteria began to creep into the judgment of biographers, the Puritan age was on the wane" (Miller and Johnson, *Puritans*, pp. 464–465. See in the same volume the general discussion of early New England biography and the selections from it, pp. 459–544).

V. "A LITTLE RECREATION OF POETRY"

1. Cotton Mather, *Manuductio ad Ministerium* (Boston, 1726), pp. 38–39.

2. *Manuductio*, p. 40.

3. *Manuductio*, p. 42:

4. *Ibid.*

5. *Manuductio*, pp. 42–43.

6. See Harold S. Jantz, *The First Century of New England Verse* (Worcester, 1944). Mr. Jantz has discovered a great deal of unpublished verse, and has reprinted some of it in his book.

7. *Handkerchiefs from Paul,* edited by Kenneth B. Murdock (Cambridge, 1927), pp. xv–xvi.

8. *Handkerchiefs from Paul,* p. xxxviii.

9. C. Mather, *Magnalia Christi Americana,* book III, part 1, chapter iii, section 1 (text from the Hartford edition, 1855).

10. London, 1626, and Boston, 1680; reprinted in *Handkerchiefs from Paul.*

11. F. O. Matthiessen, "Michael Wigglesworth, A Puritan Artist," in *New England Quarterly,* I, 492 (October 1928). The most recent reprint of *The Day of Doom* is that edited by Kenneth B. Murdock (New York, 1929).

12. Cotton Mather, *A Faithful Man, Described and Rewarded* (Boston, 1705), p. 24.

13. *The VVhole Booke of Psalmes Faithfully Translated into English Metre* (Cambridge, 1640).

14. *VVhole Booke of Psalmes,* Psalm 23.

15. *The Works of the Right Reverend Joseph Hall,* edited by Philip Wynter (Oxford, 1863), VI, 172.

16. *VVhole Booke of Psalmes,* preface.

17. Baxter, *Poetical Fragments,* p. v.

18. *Poetical Fragments,* p. iv.

19. Quoted in an unsigned review of *The Oxford Book of Christian Verse,* in *Times* (London) *Literary Supplement,* July 13, 1940.

20. *The Works of Anne Bradstreet in Prose and Verse,* edited by John H. Ellis (Charlestown, 1867), pp. 372–373.

21. *Works,* p. 404.

22. *Poetical Works of Edward Taylor,* p. 14.

23. *Poetical Works,* p. 174.

24. *Poetical Works,* p. 33.

25. *Poetical Works,* p. 107.

26. *Poetical Works,* p. 177.

27. *Poetical Works,* p. 78.

28. *Poetical Works,* pp. 165–166.

29. *Poetical Works,* p. 166.

30. *Poetical Works,* p. 43.

31. *Poetical Works,* p. 44.

32. *Poetical Works,* p. 46.

33. See Nathalia Wright's suggestive article, "The Morality

Tradition in the Poetry of Edward Taylor," in *American Literature*, XVIII (1), 1–17 (March 1946), and, in the same issue, Willie T. Weathers's "Edward Taylor, Hellenistic Puritan," pp. 18–26.

34. *Poetical Works*, p. 53.

35. *Poetical Works*, p. 61.

36. *Poetical Works*, p. 195.

37. *Poetical Works*, pp. 225–226.

38. Cotton Mather, *A Companion for Communicants* (Boston, 1690), p. 123; and Samuel Willard, *A Compleat Body of Divinity* (Boston, 1726), quoted in Taylor's *Poetical Works*, p. 28.

39. *Poetical Works*, p. 123.

40. *Poetical Works*, pp. 125, 132.

41. *Poetical Works*, p. 147.

42. Thomas H. Johnson, "Some Edward Taylor Gleanings," in *New England Quarterly*, XVI, 284 (June 1943).

43. Johnson, "Gleanings," p. 281.

44. *Poetical Works*, p. 24.

45. *Poetical Works*, p. 116.

46. *Poetical Works*, p. 15.

47. *Poetical Works*, p. 31.

VI. THE PURITAN LEGACY

1. *Boston Herald*, April 15, 1924.

2. H. K. Rowe, *History of Religion in the United States* (New York, 1924), p. 15.

3. H. W. Clark, *History of English Nonconformity* (London, 1911–1913), I, 1–19.

4. "Milton," in *The Complete Works of Ralph Waldo Emerson*, edited by E. W. Emerson (Boston, 1903–04), XII, 255.

5. *Ibid.*

6. Mather Byles, *The Glories of the Lord of Hosts* (Boston, 1740), p. 22. My attention was called to this passage, and to that referred to in note 8 below, by Mr. R. S. Carroll's unpublished essay, "Prose Style in the Sermons of Three Mathers."

7. Carroll, p. 36.

8. Mather Byles, *A Discourse on the Present Vileness of the*

Body, and Its Future Glorious Change by Christ (Boston, 1732), p. 5. In the second edition, Boston, 1771, "beautious Face" becomes "enchanting Face" (p. 10).

9. See Batsell B. Baxter, *The Heart of the Yale Lectures* (New York, 1947), pp. vii, 320, and *passim.* Cf. John Brown, *Puritan Preaching in England* (New York, 1900), the published volume of Brown's Yale lectures.

10. B. B. Baxter, ch. vii.

11. Quoted in B. B. Baxter, p. 141, from William H. P. Faunce, *The Educational Ideal in the Ministry* (New York, 1908). Cf. pp. 37 above.

12. B. B. Baxter, pp. 146–147.

13. B. B. Baxter, pp. 172–173.

14. Cabot, *Memoir of Ralph Waldo Emerson*, I, 241.

15. *The Writings of James Russell Lowell* (Riverside ed.; Boston, 1890–91), I, 380.

16. *The Writings of Henry David Thoreau* (Walden ed.; Boston, 1906), XIII, 108, 109.

17. Thomas Prince, *A Chronological History of New England* (Boston, 1736), I, xi.

18. John S. Bassett, *The Middle Group of American Historians* (New York, 1917), p. 9.

19. *Ibid.*

20. Bassett, p. 11.

21. George Bancroft, *A History of the United States*, preface to vol. I (1834).

22. Bancroft, "Introduction" in vol. I.

23. Bassett, *American Historians*, p. 181.

24. J. A. Froude, quoted in Bassett, p. 226.

25. Bassett, p. 229.

26. F. O. Matthiessen, *American Renaissance* (New York, 1941), p. 40.

27. "A Fable for Critics," in *Writings of Lowell*, IX, 51.

28. *Writings of Lowell*, IX, 85.

29. John Bunyan, "Dying Sayings," in *The Works of John Bunyan*, edited by George Offor (London, 1854), I, 65.

30. *Massachusetts Historical Society Collections*, series 5 (Boston, 1878), V, 460.

31. Quoted in Matthiessen, *American Renaissance*, p. 190.

32. Herbert W. Schneider, *The Puritan Mind* (New York, 1930), pp. 262–263.

33. Matthiessen, *American Renaissance*, p. 243.

34. *Ibid.*

35. Newton Arvin, *Hawthorne* (Boston, 1929), p. 203.

36. Henry James, *Hawthorne* (New York, 1879), p. 65; T. S. Eliot, "On Henry James," reprinted in *The Question of Henry James*, edited by F. W. Dupee (New York, 1945), p. 115. The essay originally appeared in the *Little Review* for August 1918.

37. Matthiessen, *American Renaissance*, p. 295; James, *Hawthorne*, p. 65.

38. *Journals of Ralph Waldo Emerson*, edited by E. W. Emerson and W. E. Forbes (Boston, 1909–1914), VI, 53, entry for September 21, 1841.

39. R. W. Emerson, "Boston," in *The Complete Works of Ralph Waldo Emerson*, edited by E. W. Emerson (Boston, 1903–04), XII, 188.

40. *Works of Emerson*, XII, 193.

41. *Ibid.*

42. *Works of Emerson*, XII, 197.

43. *Works of Emerson*, XII, 203.

44. *Works of Emerson*, XII, 209.

45. Arvin, *Hawthorne*, p. 65.

46. *Works of Emerson*, X, 273.

47. "Pulvis et Umbra," in *Works* (Thistle ed.; New York, 1895–1911), XV, 290.

48. Letter of Henry Adams to Oliver Wendell Holmes, January 4, 1885, in *Henry Adams and His Friends*, edited by Harold D. Cater (Boston, 1947), p. 135.

49. Samuel Sewall, *Phaenomena Quaedam Apocalyptica Ad Aspectum Novi Orbis Configurata* (Boston, 1697), p. 59.

INDEX

INDEX

Adams, Henry: on Emerson, 208; *The Education of,* 185

Addison, Joseph, 177

Addleshaw, G. W. O.: on Protestant attitude toward religious art, 16

Ames, William, on style, 50

Andrews, Lancelot, 29, 43

Anglicanism: attitude toward art and literature, 19, 20–28, 36–37, 38–39; influence of audience on writers of, 44–45; seventeenth-century, 5–6, 8; seventeenth-century literature of, 64

Arvin, Newton, on Puritanism, 197, 201

Augustine, Saint, 70; on music and ritual, 14

Bacon, Francis, 64; *Advancement of Learning,* 118; on biography, 118; on history, 69; on Renaissance, 4

Bancroft, George, 186, 187; on the United States, 187

Bassett, John S.: on Bancroft, 187; on Hutchinson, 185–186; on Motley, 187–188; on Prince, 185

Baxter, Batsell B., on sermon style, 182, 183

Baxter, Margaret, 134

Baxter, Richard, 118, 133, 182; life of his wife, 134; on Bible, 53–54; on difference between Anglican and Puritan, 44–45; on eloquence, 47–48; on harmony, 50–51; on Herbert, 149; on his own poems, 45, 52; on poetry, 51, 149; on senses, 52–56; on style, 37, 57–58

Bay Psalm Book, 146–148

Beadle, John, 101–102

Beeching, H. C., on Catholic literature, 40

Belknap, Jeremy, 186

Bernard, Richard, on sermon style, 58

Bible, 180; authority for literary art, 25–26; Genevan, 64; King James version, 4, 64, 147; Psalms, 147, 148, 177, 178; Puritan reverence for style of, 42, 43–44, 56–57; Song of Solomon, 163, 167, 169

Blount, Thomas, on "enthusiasts," 40

Bolton, Edmund, on providential element in history, 75

Book of Common Prayer, 21; Psalter, 147

Bradford, William, 78, 91, 92, 94, 133; "History of Plimouth Plantation," 78–84, 93

Bradstreet, Anne, 31, 150–152

Brown, John, 182